Hope in a Scarlet Rope

Hope in a Scarlet Rope

KINGSLEY M. BAEHR

Tyndale House Publishers, Inc.
Wheaton, Illinois

Unless otherwise stated, Scripture verses are taken from *The Living Bible,* copyright ©
1971 owned by assignment by KNT Charitable Trust. All rights reserved.

Scripture quotations marked KJV are taken from the *Holy Bible,* King James Version.

Scripture quotations marked NKJV are taken from the *Holy Bible,* New King James Version. Copyright © 1979, 1980, 1982, Thomas Nelson, Inc., Publishers.

Library of Congress Cataloging-in-Publication Data

Baehr, Kingsley M.
  Hope in a scarlet rope /   Kingsley M. Baehr.
    p.   cm. —(Bible quest)
  ISBN 0-8423-1345-1
  1. Bible stories, English.   2. Bible—Biography—Juvenile
literature.   3. Devotional calendars—Juvenile literature.
I. Title.   II. Series.
BS551.2.B25   1994   94-9000
833'.912—dc20

Printed in the United States of America

99   98   97   96   95   94
9   8   7   6   5   4   3   2

This book is dedicated to an editorial vice president (Ron Beers), a Christian boys' camp (Deerfoot Lodge), a family (my own), a Tuesday night Bible study (Veronica, Pearl, Pat, Melida, Eleanor, and Alice), and God.

To Ron Beers because he asked me to write this book.

To Deerfoot Lodge because they invited me to speak to the boys, which caused me to develop a series of messages from which this book was born—messages I gave one year when Ron Beers was a camper!

To my dear wife, Holly, who gave valuable advice and help, and who, with my sons, Benjamin and Matthew, was genuinely excited to be related to a published writer!

To my Tuesday night Bible study, who, when I tried out some of these stories on them, encouraged me to think that they might be worthwhile reading.

To God, the Author of *The Book*, from which this book is derived.

Contents

Introduction

Welcome to Bible Quest!

As you read through the stories, you will notice that this is a different sort of devotional book. Most devotions focus only on making us better people (which isn't a bad thing). Then there are Bible study books that teach us about the Bible (which isn't bad either). But if we want to do both—become better people *and* learn about the Bible—we have to read two books. This, of course, isn't necessarily a bad thing, but it does take a lot of time.

Bible Quest combines Bible study and devotional material in one convenient place. As we learn about people, places, and events in the Bible, we also read notes that help us apply what we're reading. The result? We learn about the Bible *and* learn how to be better people while reading only one book! Nifty trick, huh?

There are fifty-two readings, one for each week of the year. However, if you want to read more than one a week, that's fine. In fact, that's great! If you want to use these devotions in a weekly youth group, Bible study, or church school, that's fine. In fact, that's great! If you want to read one devotion a year until you retire, that's not fine. In fact, that's pretty wimpy!

As you read, have fun with the characters and the places they go. Maybe even picture yourself with them as their stories unfold, standing beside them as you both make great discoveries about God, Jesus, and the Bible.

Let the quest begin!

1 An Undying Belief

GENESIS 5:1-32

There is much mystery and controversy about the era in which Enoch lived. It is not my purpose in this brief story to explain it all. Even if I tried, I could not. The outstanding thing about Enoch, however, is how he *stood out* among all the rest of the people of earth's early generations. It is upon this fact that I want to concentrate. Enoch's name is discovered in the second of two back-to-back genealogies in Genesis 4–5. The first contains names of Adam's descendants through his son Cain. The second lists names of Adam's descendants through his son Seth. In Seth's genealogy there is a significant repetition, broken only by Enoch. It goes something like this: "So-and-so was this old when his son so-and-so was born . . . *and died.*" "And died" over and over again! A litany of death!

....

In the Bible, death never means the end of existence. It always means that a separation has taken place as a result of sin. In physical death, the soul and spirit are separated from the body. In spiritual death, the soul and spirit are separated from God. Sin has caused all this. Adam and Eve died spiritually the moment they disobeyed God, even though it took a long time for physical death to get its grip upon bodies that had been created to live eternally. Are we still spiritually dead even though physically alive? That separation from God can be healed by faith in Jesus Christ, who suffered separation from his Father on the cross in our place.

....

But in the middle of all that death, there is Enoch! Listen to the simple, stately beauty of the King James Version's entry regarding him in the genealogy: "And Enoch walked with God: and he was not; for God took him." No "and died"! No separation! No mention of terrible sin committed in pride, such as for Lamech, his counterpart in Cain's genealogy! (Enoch and Lamech are both the "seventh from Adam.") Instead, Enoch was in daily communion with God. As a child once put it, "One day Enoch and God were out walking. After they had gone a long way, God said to Enoch, 'We are closer to my home than yours; just come on home with me.'"

....

Can we ever understand how much God is thrilled to find people who will walk with him daily, delighting in him? Is knowing him, experiencing the power of his resurrection and the fellowship of his suffering, important enough to us to commit our lives to him? Whatever others around us may do and think, are we all-out for him? Think of what a tremendous joy it would be if God could write next to our name what he wrote about Enoch!

....

In the midst of the godless society that was on the verge of being destroyed by the great flood, Enoch maintained a single-hearted witness that pleased God (see Heb. 11:5). He even made a prophecy of a magnificent future event that was far more "future" to him than to us: "See, the Lord is coming with millions of his holy ones. He will bring the people of the world before him in judgment, to receive just punishment and to prove the terrible things they have done in rebellion against God, revealing all they have said against him" (Jude 1:14-15). Someday that judgment will occur, but before that, all those who have put their trust in Jesus Christ will be resurrected and raptured so that we will be in the "with him" group, not the "before him" ones.

One final thought. Many see in Enoch's ascension to heaven before the Flood a wonderful Old Testament illustration of the Christians' rapture to heaven before the outpouring of God's judgment on the world for its sin. Intriguing, isn't it?

....

Do we expect to be in that great number from all ages who will be caught up to meet the Lord in the air and be forever with him? On what basis? Our own efforts or the work of the Lord Jesus Christ for us on the cross? He, who was sinless, took our sin upon him that he might give us his righteousness. That is the only basis upon which we can have Enoch's experience of walking with God right on to his home in heaven!

....

2 **Super Servant!**

GENESIS 14:14; 15:1-4; 24:1-66

Eliezer was a servant. He had been born a servant, grew up a servant, and as an adult, was still a servant. But what a super servant he was! Content in his role, conducting himself honorably, conducting his business responsibly, confessing his need for God's wisdom, he was the epitome of servanthood. In fact, he is one of the best illustrations in the whole Bible of the Holy Spirit and his work! As we go through the story, see if you can notice the similarities.

....

What is our attitude toward servanthood? We live in a society that hates responsibility and loves privileges. Have we been infected by that disease? When we ask Jesus Christ to be our Savior and Lord (Master), we are saying that we are his servants. Do we behave that way, or are our attitudes and actions showing a prideful unwillingness to spend our lives serving him and others? (Phil. 2:1-5).

....

When his master, Abraham, needed him to take up arms, he did. When he was given the position of chief of servants, he accepted it and showed himself to be totally capable and trustworthy. And when Abraham needed someone for the crucially important job of finding a wife for his son Isaac, he turned to Eliezer.

Abraham did not want his son to marry a pagan girl

who worshiped idols, but since he was unable to search
for girl himself, he called Eliezer in and gave him the job.
"Go . . . to my homeland, to my relatives, and find a wife
for [Isaac] there."

....

**A marriage arranged by a servant?! How many of us would be
willing to submit to that?! Well, our system of choosing mates
certainly is not working very well—half of the marriages in
America end in divorce! Here is a suggestion: How about
allowing the Holy Spirit to choose for us? Commit this most
important decision to God and wait for his choice. Do we trust
him that much?**

....

After receiving specific instructions from Abraham and
swearing a solemn oath, Eliezer prepared for the journey.
Ten camels were needed to carry all the dowry gifts!
Travel was difficult in those days, and Eliezer would be
going a long way, back to the city of Nahor in the Haran
district, over 450 miles.

Committing himself and the success of his mission to
God, Eliezer set out, determined to succeed. Throughout
the long days of traveling, he communed with God and
sensed God's presence and direction with him. Finally one
evening he arrived at the well outside his destination just
as the women of the city came to draw water. Parking himself near the well, he prayed. "O Jehovah, the God of my
master, show kindness to my master and . . . me. . . . This is
my request: When I ask one of [the girls of the village] for
a drink and she says, 'Yes, certainly, and I will water your
camels too!'—let her be the one you have appointed as
Isaac's wife. That is how I will know."

Beauty was not a requirement in Eliezer's list, but before
he finished praying, a beautiful young woman arrived at
the well. As he opened his eyes, there she was! He made
his request and found to his delight and gratitude that she
fit the bill perfectly, with her beauty as a bonus!

....

**Respectfulness, kindness, industriousness, and willingness to
go beyond what is requested were the qualities Eliezer was
looking for in a wife for Isaac; physical beauty was not a**

consideration. Are these same qualities important to us as we also look for the mate that God may have chosen for us? Inner beauty lasts; outer beauty fades. Beautiful older people are beautiful because their beauty of character keeps shining through when bodily beauty has departed.

....

To make a long story short, the young woman, Rebekah, took Eliezer home to her father and brother, explanations were made, Isaac's worthiness as a husband was described, the dowry gifts were presented, the marriage was proposed, and Rebekah decided to accompany Eliezer back to Canaan to become the wife of Isaac, sight unseen! Eliezer's testimony regarding the charm and grace of Isaac's person and life in Abraham's household must have been completely convincing.

....

Are we such sincere and devoted servants of God that our joy and satisfaction with Jesus Christ permeates our witness to such a degree that others will be attracted to him "sight unseen"?

....

Imagine the thrill in Eliezer's heart when he and Rebekah arrived back in Canaan and found that his choice for Isaac was perfect! "She became his wife. He loved her very much, and she was a special comfort to him after the loss of his mother" is how the Bible concludes this lovely love story.

....

Imagine the thrill that the Holy Spirit will feel one day when the bride, whom he has called out of the world for Christ, will see him, enjoy the marriage supper of the Lamb with him, and be with him forever—a perfect bride "without spot or wrinkle" or any such thing! Are you a part of Christ's bride, the church? Can you look forward to that glorious face-to-face union with him in heaven one day? If not, why not? Can you not trust the testimony of his servant, the Holy Spirit, on his behalf?

....

3 A Model Mother

ExODUS 1:7–2:15a; 6:20; Acts 7:17-22; Hebrews 11:23-26

The timing could not have been worse, must have been the thought plaguing Jochebed's mind just about every waking minute. As she awoke every morning, she would glance down at her growing abdomen and wonder if her unborn baby would be a boy or a girl. How long would she be able to hide her pregnancy under her loose-flowing clothing from Pharaoh's secret service men who were keeping a list of pregnant Israelite slave women for future reference? Pharaoh's new edict to drown their newborn baby boys in the Nile was causing her great stress. How should she pray? All around her, her people were abandoning the God of Israel who seemed helpless to deliver them out of their slavery. But she would not do so! Her faith in God sustained her through the uncertain days of her pregnancy. And yet, the timing could not have been worse!

....

"As for God, his way is perfect" the Bible tells us (2 Sam. 22:31). Moses' mother had no way of knowing that as we do. She had no Bible. What was happening to her people certainly did not look perfect to her. Yet we know that she remained faithful to God. We also know that our times are in his hands (see Ps.

31:15). God's timing is also perfect. Will we continue to trust him even when it seems that his timing could not be worse?

....

The anticipated and feared day arrived. Jochebed held in her arms a magnificent baby boy! Her husband, Amram, eight-year-old Miriam, and three-year-old Aaron crowded around, delighted, cooing, and frantically shushing the little one when he screwed up his face to cry. He just could not be heard outside the house! What a turmoil of emotions filled that humble slave home that day! Jochebed knew as soon as she saw him that she would never be able to abort his life in the Nile River. Acting quickly to put their agreed-upon plan into motion, the parents hid their new son for three months. How can you hide a healthy, hungry baby boy for that long? I have no clue! But they did, and they succeeded for three months.

Then even their ingenuity was not sufficient. They had to do something else. What? I am sure Jochebed pleaded with God for an idea of what to do. Quickly it came! She took him to the Nile just as Pharaoh had ordered. She put him in the Nile River but *not* just as Pharaoh had ordered. He was in a waterproofed basket, floating gently among the papyrus reeds along the bank just a little distance from where Pharaoh's childless daughter came daily to bathe. If God was with Jochebed, her son would be saved.

"O God of my fathers, work it out, I beg you." Jochebed prayed as she went about her work. "Keep him safe, even if I have to lose him. Protect little Miriam, standing watch out there. Keep the crocodiles away. Thank you, God, for little Aaron and his hugs. I—"

"Mommy, Mommy, you'll never guess what happened!"

"What, Miriam, what?!"

"O, Mommy, Pharaoh's daughter found him—"

"She did?!"

"Yes, Mommy. How wonderful! She wants to keep him, and when I offered to find a nurse for him, she said yes! Mommy, come quickly. You are the nurse! Come, she's waiting for you!"

And that is how Jochebed's precious son was returned to

her home and heart by no less than Pharaoh's daughter herself!

....

Have you noticed how women thwarted the most powerful potentate in the world at that time? Israelite midwives defeated Pharaoh's plan to kill the baby boys. Jochebed refused to knuckle under his unrighteous edict. His own daughter apparently charmed him into an exception in her favor. And little Miriam engineered the scheme by which Moses' mother would be paid from Pharaoh's treasury for nursing her own "condemned" son! Setting ourselves against God's will never works in the long run, and we may find that we will be thwarted in our plans in a most embarrassing way!

....

Jochebed knew she would have her son for only a short time until he was weaned—maybe, if she could stretch it out, about four years. (In those days, without Gerber and other baby foods, mothers nursed their children sometimes for three or four years. In this case, I would think it was as close to four years as possible!) So she had no time to waste. She spent those early years teaching, training little Moses as much as she could. She taught him that he was an Israelite, one of God's chosen people. She taught him about Abraham, Isaac, and Jacob, who was renamed Israel and from whom their people's name had come. She taught him about God, who made the world and everything in it. She crammed his head and heart full of God and Israel.

How did she do as a teacher? About forty years later, after spending most of his life in Pharaoh's palace, being taught all the wisdom of the Egyptians and enjoying all the pleasures and treasures of that great country, Moses chose to suffer with God's people—his people—instead, and we all know the rest of the story!

9

....

Many of us became Christians before we were teens. A major reason for accepting Christ at such a young age was the witness of godly parents. They taught us about God, Jesus, and the Bible, and modeled Christianity in their lives for us to see. Take some time to thank God for your parents and their influence in your life. And while you're at it, thank your parents too. They'd love to know that they're appreciated.

....

4 The State-of-the-Art Handyman

EXODUS 31:1-11; 35:4–40:38; 2 CHRONICLES 1:1-6

Handymen sometimes get a bad rap. They often are considered to be on a lower social level by those who have specialized in head learning rather than hand learning. I have found in my daily experience, however, that I need the help of the handyman far more often than I need the help of the educated elite!

....

We need to recognize the different skills and abilities that God has given us without making judgments about whether theirs is more valuable or desirable than ours. We would probably be surprised at God's assessment of our worth. It does not depend on which talents we have but on how faithfully we use them for God's glory.

....

Bezalel ("Beez" for short) was handy, to put it mildly! Gold, silver, bronze, jewels, and wood were his babies, so to speak. He was an artist as well! And most of all, he loved God and was committed heart and soul to his work. That is why his name and that of his associate Oholiab are found in the pages of Scripture.

Beez, please notice, was a supreme artist who was without the artistic temperament. He was willing to submit his will to God. He did not consider working according to a prescribed plan beneath his abilities. He did not feel the need to branch out into uncharted artistic waters. Yet what he produced was good enough for God's presence to dwell in! Now, that is saying something!

You see, Beez was the man who oversaw the construction of that marvel of portable engineering—the Tabernacle. He personally assisted in the actual work—an overseer working *with* his workmen. Moses had received the plans for it from God, but it was Beez's job to implement them. And by the way, there was plenty of room within those plans for him to express his artistic nature.

God also gave Beez the ability to teach others the necessary skills to help in the work. Beez did not carefully guard his knowledge as some good cooks like to do with their secret recipes. No, he felt that all he had was given to him by God, so he had no right to hoard it for himself.

....

Here is what the Bible says about Beez's talents: (God speaking) "I have . . . filled him with the Spirit of God, giving him great wisdom, ability, and skill. . . ." Anything we are capable of doing to glorify God has been given to us by God. We have no right to be proud of it as though we owned it. God owns us and all our capabilities!

....

Beez's workmanship was not slapdash, haphazard, or uncaring. He did good work. It took him and his work crew about two years to build the Tabernacle, and when it was finished, every single detail was perfect. He was a true craftsman who took pride in pleasing God. He believed in these biblical principles: "Whatever you do, do well" (Eccles. 9:10) and "Do everything for the glory of God" (1 Cor. 10:31) (even though those principles were not yet written and Beez didn't even have a Bible!).

....

What quality of work characterizes our contributions in the workaday routine of our lives? Do we do our best because we

do it for God, or do we forget that goal and just get it done as quickly as possible since we have to do it?

....

One final word. Beez's Tabernacle was not mean, insignificant work. Did you know that the gold used weighed between one and two tons; the silver, between four and five tons; and the bronze, between three and four tons?! And that is to say nothing of the jewels, animal skins, weavings, fine linen, and wood! Quite a project!

....

God's tabernacle today is within his people. His presence indwells them instead of a building. Do we recognize that we are the tabernacle or temple of the Holy Spirit, and as such, are we building our lives with spiritual gold, silver, and precious stones, and with all the care that we can? We can build to God's glory or to his dishonor. May we all be Bezalels to God's credit and praise.

....

5 Hope in a Scarlet Rope

JOSHUA 2:1-24; 6:15-17, 22-25

Everyone in Jericho knew about them. As Rahab went about her work in her inn built into the city wall by the gate, she kept turning over in her head the things she had heard. These Israelites were camped just beyond the flooding Jordan River, so she and the citizens of Jericho were safe for the time being. But it was only a matter of time; then the invasion would begin. What should she do?

They were here—waiting, waiting—as though for some special signal or something. They certainly had had no trouble wiping out Sihon and Og, the kings of the Amorites, on the other side of the Jordan. They were already occupying Amorite territory. They needed to be reckoned with!

Her friends and neighbors were frightened, but as far as she could tell, they were still hoping against hope that their gods would be adequate. When she wondered out loud whether it might not be a good idea to switch allegiance to the Israelites' God, they looked at her suspiciously and stopped talking in her presence.

....

Have we ever found ourselves worrying about a threat to our peace and well-being? Why are we afraid? Do we fear that the

gods we are serving are unable or unwilling to protect and sustain us? Maybe we secretly know that they are false gods and powerless in the face of the realities of life? Maybe we are worshiping our own intelligence and abilities? Only the God of the Bible is all-powerful, ready and able to care for his children in every situation.

....

Then Rahab began thinking about her social position in society. Her reputation as a prostitute was still hanging around her neck like the proverbial albatross. She supposed her present vocation of innkeeper was too similar in nature to her former lifestyle for her neighbors to divorce the two in their thinking. She needed a new start in a new location. But more than that, she needed something or someone who could fill the void in her life. If only she could . . . but, no, there was no way. . . .

It was then that Rahab heard the knock on her door. A thrill of fear and anticipation coursed through her as she opened it to find two Israelites standing on her doorstep. She knew just about everybody in Jericho and the frequent commuters through its gates, but she had never seen these two before. Something about their mannerisms made her sure they were not her countrymen.

A quick decision made her say, "Come in, gentlemen. You shouldn't be seen in our streets. Our men will kill you because they are afraid of your people."

"How do you know who we are?"

"In my former vocation, I had to become an extremely good judge of character to protect myself. It wasn't hard to figure you out. You are spies aren't—"

Loud hammerings on the door resounded through the house.

"Quick, up on the roof. It's the king's soldiers. Hide here under this drying flax. . . . Yes, I know, it stinks, but that smell will save your life if the soldiers search the house!"

Rahab hurried downstairs, opened her door, and confronted the soldiers. She got rid of them by lying, sending them on a wild-goose chase into the mountains.

....

Should Rahab have lied to protect the spies? No, of course not. But how was she to know that? Her knowledge of God was scanty at best. She was doing what came naturally to her, considering her past. But we know better. We know that God is perfectly able to carry out his will all by himself and doesn't need us to lie to help him. Yet, have we ever lied in an effort to assist God's work?

....

Back on the rooftop, the two men slid out from under the flax at Rahab's request and then heard her say some totally unexpected words. "I know perfectly well that your God is going to give my country to you. We are all afraid of you; everyone is terrified if the word *Israel* is even mentioned. For we have heard how the Lord made a path through the Red Sea for you when you left Egypt! And we know what you did to Sihon and Og, the two Amorite kings east of the Jordan, and how you ruined their land and completely destroyed their people. Your God is the supreme God of heaven. Now I beg for this one thing: Swear to me by the sacred name of your God that when Jericho is conquered you will let me live, along with [my family] and all their families."

....

Please notice that all the people of Jericho had the same information, but only Rahab put her trust in the God of Israel. She chose to do so when everyone else (except her extended family) did not. Salvation requires us to choose to trust Christ. It is an act of the will.

....

The spies agreed, with three provisions: (1) Rahab and all her family must be in her house when the battle started, (2) they must stay there until rescued, and (3) she must leave a scarlet rope in the window to identify her house.

She let them down through a window in the wall by a scarlet rope that she left hanging in the window. Then she set about convincing her family that they must trust her and do what she said if they expected to escape with their lives.

Rahab became a citizen of Israel, married a man named Salmon, and as a reward for her faith in God, she became an ancestress of the Lord himself (see Matt. 1:5), one of God's heroines of faith (see Heb. 11:31), and an example of active faith.

6 A New Commander for Israel

JOSHUA 14:6-15; 15:13-19; JUDGES 1:9-15; 3:5-11

Eighty-five-year-old Caleb stood on the hillside looking at the men standing before him, men who had followed his lead and helped him drive out the giants from his beloved city of Hebron, his inheritance for which he had waited forty-five long years. His love was strong for his men who had been through battle together. He knew that God was with him but that the battles were not over yet. He also knew that it was time to begin handing over more responsibility to younger men. There was the small town of Debir that still needed to be captured, so it would be a good opportunity to delegate the leadership of this battle to a younger man.

....

Unlike Caleb's battles, our warfare today is not physical, directed against other human beings, it is spiritual, against Satan and lust, which war against our souls (1 Pet. 2:11). Jesus has commanded us to love our human enemies and pray for those who persecute us (Matt. 5:44), but we are also to resist the devil and he will flee from us (James 4:7). Old Testament warfare against surrounding nations, commanded by God to Israel, is only illustrative to us who live in God's day of grace (1 Cor. 10:11; Rom. 15:4).

....

His eye fell upon Othniel, and an appreciation for that young man's practical belief in God and good qualities surged warmly through him. His thoughts immediately went to Achsah, his daughter. He had noticed her interest in Othniel, and although Othniel had said nothing (being a man of action rather than words), Caleb was sure that Othniel was interested in Achsah. He had seen the glances sent her way in unguarded moments.

Suddenly an idea occurred to him that was so brilliant he could hardly believe that he had been capable of it! "Men," he shouted, "you have done a great job! The giants who frightened your parents so badly forty-five years ago are gone! God has given us the victory! Now, we need to follow up on our initial success. Debir is just over the ridge there. It needs to be taken if this hill is going to be ours. You have all followed my lead in the capture of Hebron. You know how it is done. Now, which of you will step forward and take command of the battle of Debir? And by the way, whoever does can marry my daughter Achsah if you want!"

"I want it, Caleb!" called out Othniel, quickly stepping forward and then blushing with embarrassment as his companions enjoyed a good laugh at his expense.

Caleb's smile was not because of Othniel's confusion but because his idea was working so beautifully.

Othniel did lead the attack on Debir, Debir was captured, and not long afterwards, a wedding ceremony took place.

....

What are we doing in our youth? Are we following the Calebs that we know, trying to learn from them everything we can about how to be a spiritual soldier for God? Or have we written off the old geezers as ancient and irrelevant? Are we willing and ready to volunteer our services for the Lord? How about mowing the church lawn, helping in vacation Bible school, or involving ourselves in a short-term missions project? I know two young men who found their future wives on the mission field in just such a way!

....

Years passed. Caleb had gone to his eternal reward. Israel had fallen into idolatry and then into eight years of slavery to a cruel tyrant with an impossible name,

Cushan-rishathaim. And yet, here and there, there were those who had not bowed their knees before the Baals and Asherahs that everyone else was worshiping.

Finally, it got to be too much, and the nation remembered God, who had given them the victory so many times in the good old days of Joshua and Caleb. So Israel began to cry out to God for help.

And as God looked down into the hearts of men, he saw a heart that had never deserted him, the heart of a man who had proven his worth when he was young, a man who had been willing to learn from his elders and then put what he learned into practice.

And God said, "That's my man for this crisis. I know I can use him to bring victory to Israel. I know he will trust me and not depend on his own strength and intelligence. I know because he already proved it when he was young, and he has remained true to me through all these years.

"Othniel, front and center!"

"Yes, my Lord. What will you have me to do?"

Therefore, we read: "The Spirit of the Lord took control of him, and he reformed and purged Israel so that when he led the forces of Israel against the army of King Cushan-rishathaim, the Lord helped Israel conquer him completely. Then, for forty years under Othniel, there was peace in the land."

....

How about us? Will God be able to use us in times of crisis because we have proven ourselves faithful to him in our youth? Are we willing to learn from our parents, Sunday school teachers, elders, or pastors? Will we step forward and say to God, "Here am I; send me"?

....

7 The Southpaw and the Outhouse
Part 1

JUDGES 3:12-19

Ehud was left-handed in a time when bias against lefties was strong. (Our English word *sinister,* meaning "evil, threatening," comes from the Latin word *sinistre,* meaning "on the left side.") Yet, Ehud had managed to become an important man in the tribe of Benjamin, a tribe noted for the number of left-handed men in its population. I wonder if Ehud often wished that God had made him right-handed? But God had special work for him that only a lefty could accomplish.

Have we ever wished that God had made us different from the way we are? Maybe we should be asking God to show us his reasons for creating us tall, short, big-nosed, knobby-kneed, etc., instead of complaining about it!

Ehud had the rather dubious honor of presenting the yearly tribute to fat King Eglon of Moab, who had been oppressing Israel for eighteen years. God had allowed this oppression because Israel had fallen into the worship of Moab's gods. Eglon was bad-tempered and vicious, so if the tribute displeased him, Ehud could lose his life. But so what? *One less left-handed man* is probably what the Israelites thought.

....

Other than the true God, any "god" to which we devote ourselves will take and take from us until we are destroyed. Where is the sense in worshiping money, popularity, power, music, TV, or media and sports stars? What can any of them give us that is of any eternal value? But all of them can steal from us valuable time, principles, and spiritual focus, ruining us for any worthwhile service to God. Our lives could become as bad as Israel's if we don't place God first.

....

This year, though, before he left for King Eglon's occupation headquarters in Jericho, Ehud made a dagger eighteen inches long, which he strapped on his right thigh under his outer robe. Although the Bible does not specifically say so, I think he did this under orders from God himself.

Down to Jericho he went, presented the tribute, sent his porters away, and then returned to the foot of the outside steps leading up to the patio on the roof of Eglon's house, where the king had built a specially designed chamber— complete with bathroom—to provide privacy while catching the cool afternoon breezes.

To the downstairs guards Ehud said, "I have a secret message for the king." The downstairs guards probably, at this point, checked Ehud for weapons. Seeing none, they shouted to the upstairs guards, "Ehud's back with a secret message for the king!"

When Eglon was informed by the upstairs guards that Ehud had a secret message for him, he was probably amused. There had been no trouble for eighteen years; it never occurred to him to expect it now. "Send him up, and since this is a secret message—ha, ha—all you guys can leave." Eglon shooed his attendants out; Ehud entered, shut the door, dropped to one knee with head bowed, and stretched his *right hand* forward in the properly humble position expected in a king's presence.

"But, wait," you say. "What about Ehud's dagger? Why didn't the guards discover it if they checked for weapons?"

Because Ehud was left-handed, his dagger was on his

21

right hip. Nobody ever strapped a dagger on his right hip because no army commander in his right mind would allow lefties in his army. They were trouble. They were in league with the devil. They would jinx any chance for victory. So the guards never thought to frisk Ehud's right hip, much to their later regret.

....

Carelessness is often very costly. Underestimating the enemy can be disastrous. Our enemy Satan is powerful, clever, and deceptive. Many Christians have experienced times of relative comfort and well-being and have been lulled into carelessness in the fight against Satan. Instead of resisting him, they begin playing with him, enjoying his subtle attractions. We need to be on guard by putting on the whole armor of God (Eph. 6:10-17). (While Eglon is the bad guy in this story, we can still learn from his mistakes.)

....

8 The Southpaw and the Outhouse
Part 2

JUDGES 3:20-30; 4:1

"So, you have a secret message for me." Eglon leaned forward in mock interest.

"Yes, from the God of Israel," Ehud responded.

Eglon arose from his reception room throne, probably saying something like, "Oh, I thought I was the god of Isr—" But he never finished his sentence.

Ehud, still bowing (he no doubt had practiced this move over and over), grabbed the haft of his dagger from his right hip with his left hand, his right hand still stretched out, and in one fluid motion drove it upward into Eglon's belly and into his heart. Eglon died instantly. No time to call out for help, sinking to the floor, the oppressor of God's people would afflict them no more.

....

We are commanded by God to put to death the "Eglons" in our lives. For example, Colossians 3:5 lists fornication, uncleanness, passion, evil desire, and covetousness as some "Eglons" that we are to ruthlessly rid ourselves of. Are we, like Ehud, willing to cut out of our lives those things that rob us of victory and joy in the Lord?

....

Ehud left the reception room, locked the doors behind him, and escaped to gather his army. They took control of the fords of the Jordan River located between Jericho and Moab.

Meanwhile, back at Eglon's rooftop chamber the king's servants waited and waited to be summoned by their lord. Since he was in his private chambers, they did not dare to enter uninvited in case he was using his bathroom "throne."

Finally, they could wait no longer. They unlocked the doors, peeked in, and saw their king in a heap on the floor, blood and guts much in evidence. The news spread quickly through the Moabite army in Jericho, and lacking a commander, they ran for home, crossing the ford in the Jordan River. Here Ehud's waiting band of patriots easily picked off the enemy army.

The Moabite domination was ended, Israel served the Lord during the eighty remaining years of Ehud's long life, and he became the man God used to judge his people wisely.

....

We tend to think of God as the God of the universe, holding the whole creation together by the word of his power, and forget that he is also the God of the commonplace and mundane. If God can use a king's outhouse in his planning, surely there is nothing too insignificant for his attention and involvement.

....

9 The Fearless Farmer

JUDGES 3:31; 4:1-3, 6-7

Midnight. A silent, single file of Philistines slips along the path toward an Israelite border farm, intent on raiding, looting, and burning, then capturing potential Israelite slaves.

Suddenly, a scream! Then silence. The Philistines stop, shaken, peering into the darkness. A whisper: "Last man's down—again." They do not even check out their fallen comrade. They know what has happened. The phantom has found them and struck again. They race for home. The dead man lies in the path with a round stab wound in his back.

What is the count now? Approaching six hundred dead Philistine raiders! *How does he find us? How does he know where we will raid next? What weapon is he using?* Night after night, all along the Philistine-Israelite border, the phantom has been at work, saving Israel from the incursions of the Philistine raiders. *Who is he? Does anyone know his name?*

The eyes of Israel had been focused for years on the Megiddo Valley and the northern hills where Sisera and his nine hundred iron chariots had been terrorizing the Israelites, forcing them to pay exorbitant taxes and bribes to keep King Jabin of Canaan appeased.

The Philistines in the southwest thought they saw a golden opportunity for raiding since Israel's manpower and resources were being occupied northward. Then they encountered the phantom.

25

....

It is a rare thing today that a single person is willing to get involved in keeping evil in check at great personal danger and sacrifice. Not many of us will involve ourselves in helping others, even when there is no personal danger! Are we fighting the forces of Satan by doing what we can to ward off their attacks on our fellow believers? The "phantom" was!

....

In an Israelite farmhouse, Shamgar dragged himself off his mat and rolled it up for the new day. The mornings came too quickly these days. His farm reflected his weariness. In fact, when his good friend and neighbor dropped by at dusk that day, he finally decided to voice something that had been on his mind for quite some time.

"Sham, old buddy, what is it with you? You look wiped out, and you're in the prime of your life! Your farm is going to pot. What's going on? Come on, you can tell me."

"I am just getting old, friend. I can't sleep much nights anymore. You know what they say about old folks and insomnia."

Later, as Shamgar's friend walked home, a lightbulb suddenly flashed on over his head. Could it be? Could it really be? He had heard about the phantom. Maybe his own farm had been protected one night by Sham. He himself had felt guilty sometimes that it was not he out there on the front lines. But Shamgar? Yes! It all fit! His tiredness, his neglected farm, his secretiveness, his character! He was the type—a man of action, of few words. And yes, his ox goad would make round wounds! It had to be Shamgar! Shamgar was the phantom!

What a scoop! He had to tell everybody. Shamgar never would. But wait! If he told, the Philistines would eventually find out, and it would be curtains. He couldn't tell, at least not yet. But if the enemy ever stopped its raiding, then and only then would he tell. He would make sure everyone knew what a hero his friend was!

....

Shamgar was not a trained soldier like the Philistines; he was just a farmer. He had no proper military weapon—only an ox goad. He could have made excuses. Instead he made a differ-

ence! He could have done nothing, but under God's direction, he delivered Israel! What deliverance can God use us to accomplish for him?

....

Author's Note: The friend and Shamgar's method for delivering Israel are purely out of my imagination, but I think they could explain the facts pretty well.

10 The Hijacker's History
Part 1

JUDGES 10:6–11:27

Jephthah (we will call him "Jep") had two strikes against him before he even saw the light of day. He had been conceived during his father's sexual sin with a prostitute. Then because his father had sired other sons by his own wife and then had the nerve to bring Jep into the family, Jep's half brothers hated him, seeing him as an additional claimant on the family fortune.

But apparently the only person who could have and did teach Jep what little knowledge of God that she had was his father's wife! No one else seemed to have cared enough about God or Jep to have done so. As they grew older, the animosity against Jep increased to the point that his half brothers threw him out of their home territory of Gilead and told him never to return. So Jep went to Tob, a wild, deserted area of the northern Arabian desert, and made a living leading a band of hijackers who preyed on camel caravans traveling through the region.

Several years passed. Back in Gilead things were not going well at all. The fierce Ammonites were threatening to invade, and no Gileadite was willing to take the leadership against them. Finally, in desperation they sent a delegation to Jep to ask him to return and lead the men of Gilead into battle if necessary.

"Why should I?" muttered Jep. "You threw me out, remember? Why should I help a bunch of wimps like you?"

"We will make you governor of Gilead if you are successful."

"Sure you will! . . . You will? You're not just putting me on?"

"Yes, we will, as God is our witness," the wimps grumbled, hating what they were being forced to do.

"You got a deal," said an exultant Jep. He then began making plans to return.

....

Jep was not ideal material for God to use as a deliverer of his wayward people in this latest crisis, and yet God was going to use him. He was rough, embittered, and lived by the law of the gang he led—No favors; you scratch my back, then I'll scratch yours. On the other hand, none of us are ideal material either, yet God has chosen to use us in his battle against Satan. We need to recognize God's sovereignty in these matters and avoid becoming proud of our position in Christ, as though we had somehow earned it by our worthiness. We also must remember that no matter what our past God is still able to use us if we are willing to live for him in the present.

....

Back to Mizpah, a major city in Gilead, they went, and we read that Jep uttered all his words before the Lord there! A remarkable statement about someone such as he! Apparently, his early indoctrination about God at his stepmother's knee had remained with him (at least in part), and he knew that success in the coming confrontation rested in the hope of God's power and help.

But, surprisingly, before taking action against Ammon, Jep tried diplomacy. And again we see that somewhere, sometime, he had been taught something of the history of God's people because the message he sent to the king of Ammon was full of accurate knowledge of God's dealings with Israel.

11 The Hijacker's History
Part 2

JUDGES 11:28–12:7; HEBREWS 11:1-2, 32-33

Diplomacy did not work. The Ammonite king was looking for a fight. Facts and reason were worthless to him. So the men of Gilead under Jep's leadership prepared for battle.

And so did Jep. *He made a vow to God.* He did not have to make a vow—God was going to give him the victory anyway. But Jep's knowledge of God's ways was scanty and faulty. He thought that to get God to do something for him, he had to do something for God—you know, You scratch my back, then I'll scratch yours—the law of the gang.

....

Knowing God well is vital to Christians. It will save them from making the kinds of mistakes Jep made that come from thinking God is something he is not. The Word of God is the best place to find the knowledge of God. Are we studying it diligently every day?

....

Yes, Jep made a vow to God. It changed his life!

He said, "If You will indeed deliver the people of Ammon into my hands, then it will be that whatever comes out of the doors of my house to meet me, when I return in peace from the people of Ammon, shall surely be the LORD's, *and I will offer it up as a burnt offering.*" Oh, Jep, what have you done?!

....

Have we ever tried to force God into doing what we want by making deals with him? "If you will only help me pass this test, I promise to study hard for the next." "If you will only help me find a better-paying job, I promise that I will give you 15 percent instead of 10." Etc. If we are asking according to his will, he will give freely; we do not have to "scratch his back"!

....

God gave Jep the victory. As he approached his house, the door flew open, and running to greet him was not the ox, sheep, or goat he was expecting (yes, animals often lived in the houses with the people in those days) but his one and only child, his daughter, whom he loved with all his heart.

Jep tore his clothes, and cried out, "Alas, my daughter! You have brought me to the dust. For I have made a vow to the Lord and I cannot take it back." Notice that he said "cannot," not "will not." Do you see the significance? Jep was such a man of his word that it was impossible for him to break his vow.

....

We live in a society where our word means nothing. People think nothing of lying in order to get their way. God says in Psalm 15:4 that one characteristic of a person who can stand in his presence is that he vows to his own hurt but does not change it. Broken contracts, broken marriage vows, broken promises are all around us. Are we like Jep, who could not break his vow?

....

What happened? Jep carried out his vow with his daughter. There are two schools of thought here: (1) He sacrificed her to the Lord as a burnt offering, and (2) he dedicated her to the Lord as a perpetual virgin. I am sure that the first is the correct one because his reaction when he saw her was too grief stricken to be explained by the second; his overreaction to the complaints of the Ephraimites soon after can only be explained by the first; and his untimely death only six years later while he was still in the prime of life seems to be explained by a broken heart and loss of the will to live.

Was God pleased with what Jep did? Yes and no. Yes, because he kept his word. No—a thousand times no—because he sacrificed his daughter. His reason for what he did delighted the heart of God. What he did was a horror to God.

....

God is able to distinguish between our motivations and our actions. If we were to withhold judgment of a person's actions until we knew what his motives were, we would save ourselves much embarrassment and unnecessary concern and trouble.

....

You might be surprised to know that Jep is enshrined in God's Hall of Faith in Hebrews 11:32. Jep? A man of faith? Oh yes! Faithful to his vow because he truly believed God had given him the victory. Faithful to his concept of God (though faulty) even though it cost him his daughter's life.

....

May God find us to be people of faith and integrity like Jep but with clearer knowledge of his perfect character.

....

12 You and Me against the World

1 SAMUEL 9:15-17; 13:1-22; 14:1-23

Saul's situation was desperate. The ferocious Philistines were threatening again, his "national guard" of three thousand men was deserting him, and he had just been judged by God himself for abusing his power as king. Only six hundred men remained with him, and they were trembling in fear. Even though God had promised that Saul would deliver his people from the Philistine menace, all confidence in their king had disappeared.

But Jonathan, Saul's son and commander of one contingent of the army, still had confidence in God. As day after day passed, he watched his father sitting on his hands, bemoaning the depleted numbers of his fearful followers. Finally, Jonathan could stand it no longer. God had promised victory, so he was going to believe God and take action.

....

We face spiritual Philistines every day. They may appear large, menacing, and unconquerable. But God has promised us victory over them. Do we trust him enough to take action against them, calling on him for the necessary courage and strength?

....

Jonathan called his armor-bearer aside. (Armor-bearers were men chosen by military leaders as their adjutants. They carried armor, acted as bodyguards, and were couriers when needed. They were considered to be highly dependable and trustworthy.) What Jonathan said to him can be expressed by this poem:

"The Lord is not limited," Jonathan cried,
"By how few we are or by host multiplied.
It's possible we can be used by the Lord—
So, let's go and ambush that Philistine horde!"

"That's crazy!" we say—"such impossible odds!"
But is it? The Lord versus Philistine gods?
The Lord, with the pow'r to create you and me,
Versus gods made of stone or of crudely carved tree?

....

Why is it that we are so often confused
And let the majority keep us bemused,
And we follow them blindly, unable to see
That one on God's side is a majority?

....

Now if you were Jonathan's armor-bearer, how would you respond to such a suggestion? Just the two of you against a whole Philistine garrison! A suicide mission! And yet, hear the answer of the armor-bearer: "Fine! Do as you think best; I'm with you heart and soul, whatever you decide."

....

Leaders need loyal followers. Can our spiritual leaders count on our support as they step out in faith to engage the foe? Even when it seems that, humanly speaking, the venture is risky? We may never realize how much such support is appreciated, but to the leaders it is invaluable.

....

The results? Details are available in 1 Samuel 14:8-22. As Jonathan and his armor-bearer stepped out in faith, God stepped in, took over, routed the Philistines, and the rest of Israel's fainthearted army even participated in the mop-up operations. "So the Lord saved Israel that day."

....

The honor goes to God, the faith in action comes from us, and the whole company of believers reaps the blessings! Not bad, considering it all started with two men! May we as leaders or "armor-bearers" team up with our counterparts and win victories for God's honor and glory and for the blessing of our Christian communities.

....

13 The Gospel according to Bo
Part 1

2 SAMUEL 4:4; 9:1-13

Mephibosheth ("Bo" for short) had royal blood flowing through his veins, but you would never have known it to look at him. His grandfather had been King Saul, the first king of Israel, and his father had been Jonathan, King David's closest friend.

Yes, Bo was royalty, and as our story begins, he had a rightful claim to the throne, humanly speaking. But Bo's royal line had been rejected by God because of the disobedience of his grandfather, Saul (1 Sam. 15:26).

When the news of the deaths of Saul and Jonathan arrived back home, Bo's nurse, thinking that Bo might be executed by the new king (she did not know how kind David was), hastily gathered a few belongings together and fled with Bo. Maybe they started out running, but shortly the nurse felt that Bo was not able to run fast enough, so she picked him up under one strong arm and hurried on.

Well, no self-respecting five-year-old wants to be carried by his nurse—he wants to do it himself! So Bo struggled to free himself from that arm, and in the process his nurse dropped him. He landed somehow on his spine and became paralyzed from the waist down, never to walk again.

Bo's family's holdings had, by law, become the property of the new king, so he was destitute. Poor Bo became a charity case, dependent for life upon the kindness of a merciful man named Machir, who took the boy into his home, where Bo grew to adulthood.

And to make things worse, Bo never knew when King David might find him and summon him to the palace to be executed. In those days, you see, execution of the old royal family was standard procedure. It prevented any possibility that they might try to regain the throne. So Bo lived under constant fear of death.

....

Believe it or not, we have many things is common with Bo. (1) We are royalty too: God created the human race to be rulers of his earthly creation (Gen. 1:26-28). Our royal line has also been rejected by God because of the disobedience of our ancestor Adam (Rom. 5:12-14). (2) In the Bible lameness is often symbolic of the debilitating effects of sin in our lives, making us unable to walk in the path of God's will and unfit for God's presence (Lev. 21:18-23). (3) The fear of death is upon us as well (John 3:36; Heb. 2:15) since the wages of sin is death (Rom. 6:23). (4) Also we are charity cases, living only by the mercy of God, completely unable to buy his favor since all our righteousnesses are only filthy rags in his sight (Isa. 64:6). Suddenly Bo doesn't look so pitiful, or we don't look so great, right?

....

Years passed. Then one day the dreaded summons came. A messenger arrived accompanied by several soldiers with the king's command that Bo present himself at court. I wonder if, in the midst of his fear, Bo was not almost glad that it had finally come to a head and the years of dreadful waiting were ended.

As Bo entered the throne room, he bowed deeply to King David, showing as much humility as was possible for him. He hardly dared look up at the face of the king.

"Mephibosheth?" The voice was not what Bo expected. It was gentle, kind, with something of a deep sorrow in it.

"I am your servant," Bo replied, touching his forehead to the floor.

"Don't be afraid! I've asked you to come so that I can be kind to you because of my vow to your father, Jonathan. I will restore to you all the land of your grandfather, Saul, and you shall live here at the palace!"

....

We don't have to remain in our pitiful spiritual shape. Changing depends on how we react to the mercy and grace of God. Bo could have taken the attitude of many people that they do not need or want God's mercy: They are the "masters of their own fate and captains of their own souls," and where does God get off offering them charity! They are doing very well on their own, thank you, so God should butt out! Obviously that attitude will get them nowhere with God. It is only by accepting his mercy and the work of Christ on the cross that we will live together with him in his palace in the heavenly kingdom.

....

Bo could hardly believe what he had just heard. No condemnation, no death sentence, not even prison! Instead, favor, restoration of property, adoption into the royal family, and servants to serve him!

"Should the king show kindness to a dead dog like me?" was Bo's dazed reply.

Bo discovered that David was as good as his word, and Bo became a happy member of David's household with all its rights and privileges.

14 The Gospel according to Bo

Part 2

2 SAMUEL 16:1-4; 19:24-30; 21:1-7

More time passed. Absalom, David's third son, was marching on Jerusalem to take over the kingdom. David was hurrying into exile. Bo asked his servant Ziba for a donkey he could ride to go with David, who had given him so much. But Ziba, seeing an opportunity for self-advancement, used the donkey to bring food to David, leaving Bo behind. Ziba told David that Bo had stayed behind hoping to take the kingdom for himself during the turmoil. David did not have time to investigate the truth of Ziba's words, so he turned over to Ziba all of Bo's property.

....

Our King is perfect, knowing the end from the beginning, able to see into men's hearts. We need never fear that he will misjudge us or make mistakes.

....

Several months later Absalom was dead, killed in battle, and David was returning to Jerusalem in triumph. One of the first to meet him as he crossed the Jordan River was Bo. But what a mess he was! He had not trimmed his beard, washed his clothes, or cared for his feet during the whole time David had been gone. David probably smelled him before he saw him.

Why didn't Bo take care of himself? He was in mourning and wanted everyone to know it. He could not follow David physically, so he followed him in his heart. He identified himself with David the only way he could: symbolically. Everyone in Absalom's court knew whose side Bo was on! He took no part in the revelry. He was "in the world, but not of it." His king had been rejected, and he would have no part of the usurper's reign.

....

Do people know who our King is? Are we so much a part of the world in which we live that people cannot see any difference? I am not suggesting that we have to make ourselves offensive to maintain a testimony for Christ, but we do have to be willing to separate ourselves from those things in the world that dishonor his holy name.

....

"Why didn't you come with me, Bo?" asked David.

Then the truth came out and presented David with a dilemma. What could he do and still maintain his dignity? Finally he said, "Bo, you and Ziba can divide the property."

Bo's answer is a classic. "Give him all of it. I am content just to have you back again!"

Some time later, David found it necessary to turn over to the Gibeonites seven members of Saul's family to atone for Saul's sins. They were executed by the Gibeonites. All the reasons for this are too complicated for the limits of this story, but the key fact is that Bo was exempted from this retribution. He remained secure in David's family where the judgment that fell on his relatives could not touch him.

....

The day is coming when God is going to pronounce and execute judgment on all who are not members of his family (Jude 1:14-15). Do you enjoy the eternal security of knowing that God is your Father, or will you face God as your righteous Judge and Executioner one day? Bo has illustrated to us the way of salvation. Will we accept it for ourselves? Will we tell others of this way?

....

15 Quality in Crisis

2 SAMUEL 6:1-15; 1 CHRONICLES 13:1-14; 15:1-28;
6:1-6, 37-38; 26:4-8

As David looked around, seething with anger, he saw the house just there by the side of the road. He strode up to the door, banged on it belligerently, and waited. When Obed-edom saw the king of Israel banging on his door, he broke away from the crowd of onlookers, hurried up to David, and said, "O King, this is my house. May I serve you?"

"I need a place to put that dangerous Ark for a while. Your house is convenient. I order you to keep it until I can figure out what to do with it!"

"Certainly, my lord, O King. I am a Levite from the city of Gath-rim-mon in the tribe of Dan. I would be honored to have the Ark of the Covenant under my humble roof."

"Be careful, man. Did you see what just happened to Uzzah? All he did was reach out to steady the Ark on the cart when the oxen stumbled, and God struck him dead! I don't get it! He was trying to help, and he gets zapped for his trouble! I'm afraid of God today. I thought I knew what God was like, but this—I just don't know."

"That's OK, my lord. I have a spare room where we can put it until further orders."

"Good, good. By the way, what's your name?"

"Obed-edom, my lord."

"Obed-edom, huh. All right, Obed-edom, I'll remember this."

....

If we have the opportunity to be of service to our fellow Christians, are we willing servants, even if there might be some risk involved? Do others feel that they can call on us at any time of need without making previous arrangements with us? Also, notice that Obed-edom did not criticize David for his careless handling of the Ark. We would do well to be like Obed-edom and not criticize and berate others for their mistakes but treat them with respect and show them by example what to do.

....

Obed-edom, and eventually even David, discovered that proper respect and reverence for God and his holiness result in great blessing.

The Bible tells us that "the Lord blessed Obed-edom and all his household" during the three months that he respectfully housed the Ark of the Covenant. And it was not long before David heard about it. By that time, he had time to think about how Obed-edom had handled the Ark as it was being transferred from the road to his home. David realized that he was responsible for the tragic ending to his first attempt to bring the Ark to the special tent he had prepared for it. He decided to try again—the right way, with the Levites carrying the Ark by its poles. This time the transfer from Obed-edom's house to the Ark-tent was accomplished successfully and with great joy and celebration.

....

We need to serve the Lord in the Lord's prescribed way. Our ideas of how things should be done should not be borrowed from the world, as David borrowed his cart idea from the Philistines (1 Sam. 6:10-11). Our inspirations should come from God's Word, the Bible.

....

King David was no dummy. He knew enough to make Obed-edom one of the gatekeepers—or guards—

at the Ark-tent to make sure that no one else would make the mistake of treating the Ark of the Covenant in a casual, uncaring manner. When he encountered quality, David was wise enough to put it to good use. Obed-edom was quality!

16 Benaiah—3; The World/ Flesh/ Devil—0

2 SAMUEL 8:18; 20:23; 23:20-23; 1 KINGS 1:38-40; 2:25-46;
1 CHRONICLES 11:22-25; 18:17; 27:5-6

....

"The world, the flesh, and the devil" is a well-known phrase that
lists the three enemies of the Christian. They must be fought and
defeated if he expects to live a victorious life for Christ.

....

Benaiah ("Ben" from now on) was the leader of the Cherethites and Pelethites, King David's "secret service men," or personal bodyguards. He had earned that position because he was a "heroic soldier" (2 Sam. 23:20). With God's help he had proven himself capable of victory against anything that might constitute a danger to David or himself. Three very interesting examples of his successes were chosen by the Holy Spirit to be recorded in the pages of Scripture.

First, Ben killed two lionlike men of Moab. The Moabites were indulgers of the fleshly appetites, who would rather seduce you into sin than use force. They had used their priestess-prostitutes to lure the men of Israel into idolatry (Num. 25:1-3). In another instance, one of their kings is described as a very fat man (Judg. 3:17) who required a payoff in produce from Israel every year for eighteen years. Later, Moabite women are mentioned first in the list of

those who turned King Solomon's heart away from God
(1 Kings 11:1).

....

**Moabites represent for us the appetites of our sinful natures
that war against the soul (1 Pet. 2:11). They stalk us, spring on
us when we least expect them, and rip our Christian testimo-
nies to shreds—like the lionlike men of Moab. Ben defeated
them. How good are we at using the power God has made
available to us to defeat these sinful desires? "Fleeing" them
is recommended when we feel them coming (2 Tim. 2:22), but
when they suddenly confront us, Colossians 3:1-5 gives some
clues on how we can overcome them.**

....

Next, Ben killed a lion in a pit on a snowy day! Can you
imagine even entering a pit with a lion in it? And on a slip-
pery, snowy day yet! Why this particular lion was in that pit
and why it needed killing is left up to our imagination, but
in spite of the danger, the poor visibility, the unsure foot-
ing, and the close quarters, Ben rendered that lion totally
ineffective!

....

**The devil is described in 1 Peter 5:8 as one who "prowls
around like a hungry, roaring lion, looking for some victim to
tear apart." There is a great deal of uncertainty and unclarity
in fighting the devil. He is called the father of lies (John 8:44),
the deceiver (Rev. 12:9), and the enemy (1 Pet. 5:8). He can
even transform himself into an angel of light (2 Cor. 11:14).
But he can be defeated, even though he is as close to us as our
minds. James 4:7 informs us that by submitting ourselves to
God, we can resist the devil and thus render him totally
ineffective!**

....

Finally, we read that Ben killed a gigantic Egyptian with
the Egyptian's own spear. Can you picture what that battle
must have been like—Ben parrying with his staff the furious spear thrusts of the giant (he was seven and a half feet
tall) until, with a sudden twisting motion, Ben knocked
the spear away, grabbed it, and ended the onrushing Egyptian's attack!

....

**In the Bible, Egypt is a picture of the world system with all its
"pleasures" that has set itself against God and his people. The**

pharaoh of Moses' time hardened his heart against God. Moses refused to enjoy the passing pleasures and treasures of Egypt, choosing to suffer with God's people who were called out of Egypt, just as we have been called out of the world (2 Cor. 6:14-18) and told not to love it (1 John 2:15-17). Moses' staff was used to defeat Egypt's king; Ben's, to defeat Egypt's champion; and ours? What would our staff be? It would be needed for defense, protection, and comfort in our worldly society that is attacking our ears, eyes, and minds constantly. What else could it be but the Lord's strength, provided by the Word of God as we become proficient in defensive maneuvers through constantly practicing obedience to it.Ben illustrated victorious Christian living! We can experience the same as we wield the Word of God.

....

17 Devoted to Duty

2 SAMUEL 11:1-17; 23:39; 1 CHRONICLES 11:41

....

Have we ever been given special favors by our teachers or employers that our classmates or fellow workers have not enjoyed? Have these favors made us a little suspicious as to why we were receiving them? Have our superiors released us from duties that others on our same level of employment must continue to perform? How should we handle such situations? Read on to see how one man did it.

....

Uriah was of Hittite roots, but as one of King David's officers in the army of Israel, he had adopted his Israelite name meaning "My Light is the Lord." David had found him to be absolutely honorable and a devoted military man. Few armies in those days had foreigners as officers, but Uriah was just such a man.

He also had a gorgeous wife named Bathsheba. They lived in a home near the royal palace in Jerusalem. Because he was a soldier, Uriah often had to be away from home with the army. One spring David sent his army out to fight the Ammonites under General Joab's leadership. David remained behind. He should have been leading his army as a warrior-king, but he stayed home. What happened as a result is the well-known story of David and Bathsheba's adulterous liaison. Uriah was doing his duty; David was not.

....

There will be times when it seems to us that sin is rewarded and righteousness is punished. Are we able to trust God enough to do the right thing anyway, knowing that eventually everything will be sorted out and sin will be punished and righteousness rewarded?

....

When David received Bathsheba's message that she was pregnant, David sank to an even lower level in his chosen sinful course. He decided that he had to cover up his adultery by making Uriah think the baby was his. Under the pretext of inquiring about the progress of the battle, he sent for Uriah posthaste. When Uriah arrived, David asked his hypocritical questions, and then said something like this: "Uriah, old buddy, you must be awfully tired. Why don't you go on home to your wife tonight and spend some quality time with her. Tell her I'll send dinner over so she doesn't have to cook. Tomorrow you can return to your military duties. Enjoy!"

So Uriah made a beeline for Bathsheba, right? *Wrong!* He hung out all night in the servants' quarters of the palace. When David found out that his clever cover-up had failed, he called for Uriah and asked him point-blank, "Why didn't you go home to your wife last night after being away for so long?"

Listen carefully to Uriah's answer and put yourself in David's shoes as he heard these words: "The Ark [meaning God's Presence] and the armies and the general and his officers [but not the commander-in-chief, David] are camping out in open fields, and should I go home to wine and dine and sleep with my wife? I swear that I will never be guilty of acting like that." He would not accept special favors that he felt he did not deserve. And David had taken special favors that he definitely did not deserve!

....

Are we continually looking for excuses to take liberties with the duties God has assigned to us, or, like Uriah, do we have a high sense of responsibility that won't allow such thinking?

....

David, his conscience dulled by deliberate sin, tried again by causing Uriah to become drunk, probably using a potion of some sort. He hoped to remove from Uriah his high sense of right and wrong through drink. But once again, failure. Uriah collapsed in the servants' quarters one more time.

In desperation David bottomed out. He arranged for Uriah to be placed in the forefront of the hottest battle in order that he might be killed by enemy arrows. Uriah, gallant to the end, met his death. David subsequently married Bathsheba and seemed to get away scot-free with his dreadful succession of sins. Uriah's death was quick. And David's? He died for the rest of his life as he saw his family fall into the most awful sins of lust, incest, immorality, and murder—all because of his example. David died a thousand deaths before he died. Because he eventually repented of his sins and asked God's forgiveness, God was gracious to David, but, oh, how he suffered during his lifetime!

....

Uriah could hold his head high even as he died. David could never forget the depths to which he fell because he continually saw what he had done expanded and multiplied in his family. True, God forgave him, but David still had to live with the consequences of his deeds. May God preserve us from those sins that ruin our reputations and cause our memories to be full of regret.

....

18 Bloom Where You Are Planted

2 SAMUEL 15:13-15, 23-29, 35-36; 17:15-16

B ehold, my lord, here we
are!"

"Zadok! Abiathar! You have
the Ark of God! What are you
doing here with this?"

"You went to so much
trouble to get the Ark
to Jerusalem,
my lord, that we
thought you would
want it with you in
exile. We and our Levite
servants here are ready
to go with you. Just lead the
way as you used to do so long ago when King Saul was
chasing you."

David looked fondly at the two priests. *They have been
with me through thick and thin, especially Abiathar,* thought
David, and then that long-remembered massacre of Abiathar's family stabbed his heart again. It had been his own
fault. And even though he knew that God and Abiathar
had forgiven him, he could not forgive himself. Now here
was Abiathar, faithful as ever, and dear Zadok, ready for
anything that might be coming. How he wished he could
have kept them with him!

....

**It takes great grace to be able to forgive former wrongs
against us by our fellow Christians. In fact, it takes God's grace**

to be able to do it. Abiathar could; can we? God forgave us our great wrongs against him. Can we do less than forgive others when they have wronged us?

....

"Friends, listen to me. The Ark belongs in Jerusalem. That is the city where God's presence has chosen to dwell. You men have been appointed as caretakers of the Ark. Your place is, therefore, also in Jerusalem. Please, take the Ark back with you and resume your responsibilities as priests. God wants you there. I don't know whether I will ever get back or not, but in the meantime, be my eyes and ears there, will you? Send word to me by your sons of anything you think I should know. I need you there more than here. Go with my blessings."

....

Have we ever felt that we would like to get involved in a different kind of service for God in a different place? Have we felt restless doing the same thing day after day? I am not suggesting that this is the way Zadok and Abiathar felt, but what is God's answer to us likely to be when we feel like that? It usually will be the same as David's: "Bloom where you are planted. Don't try to transplant yourself." If the Divine Gardener wants us in a different part of his garden, he will do the transplanting.

....

What did Zadok and Abiathar do? Did they pout? Argue? Quit in anger, leave the Ark, and stride off in a huff? No, they returned to Jerusalem with the Ark, resumed their daily duties, and became valuable informants for David.

....

What is our reaction if our church leaders advise us to continue serving in our present capacity when we want to do something we think will be more exciting, more challenging, more public, etc.? I hope we have the humility and grace to respond as Zadok and Abiathar did.

....

51

19 A Lesson in Loyalty— Ittai

2 SAMUEL 15:1-23; 18:1-2

Pandemonium! King David's court was in chaos! Courtiers running everywhere, servants shouting at each other, clothes and travel gear being packed! And yet, beneath it all was a sense of order. In the space of twenty-four hours, David organized several thousand of his devoted followers as they moved toward the Jordan River, hoping to cross it into exile.

What had caused this sudden disruption of palace life in Jerusalem? A messenger had arrived with the tragic news that Absalom, David's third son, had mustered an army in Hebron (about twenty miles away as the crow flies) and was planning to march on Jerusalem and wrest the kingdom from his father. Several months earlier, he had informed his father that he was going to Hebron to pay his vows to the Lord. David had been thrilled that this wayward son was finally showing some spiritual interest! And now this! David's heart was broken; yet he realized that if he stayed and fought, there would be unnecessary bloodshed. So a grieving king and the loyal core of his army and servants left Jerusalem twenty-four hours after the messenger arrived.

....

How is it with us and our parents recently? Are we a cause of joy and delight to them or of grief and tears?

....

"But," you say, "I thought this story was about somebody named Ittai?"

Well, read what 2 Samuel 15:19-20 says: "The king turned to Ittai, the captain of the six hundred Gittites [Gittites were Philistines from Gath, which had been Goliath's hometown before David killed him], and said to him, 'What are you doing here? Go on back with your men to Jerusalem, to your king, for you are a guest in Israel, a foreigner in exile. It seems but yesterday that you arrived, and now today should I force you to wander with us, who knows where? Go on back and take your troops with you, and may the Lord be merciful to you.'"

Let us try to figure this out. Here are 600 Philistines from Gath led by Ittai, leaving Jerusalem with David after having arrived only the day before. Remember, Philistines were among Israel's worst enemies, and yet the 601 Philistines follow David into exile!

When they had arrived in Jerusalem, they had not expected what they found. They were expecting to join their forces with those of an established, secure, and powerful king. Now he is running away! Is it any wonder that David counseled Ittai to take his men back to Jerusalem and support Absalom? What did David have to offer them? Hardship, uncertainty, no perks, no future. Why should they suffer with him when they were expecting to enjoy a stable court life?

....

David was concerned about others when his own life was in disarray. Does his example of unselfish caring mean anything to us? How unselfish are we when our lives are falling apart? Or do we expect everyone around us to focus on us and our troubles and come running to our aid?

....

Ittai had a choice: (a) to suffer hard times with God's

53

designated king, or (b) to enjoy the expected easy living with the usurper Absalom.

....

Which are we choosing today: to suffer with a rejected Christ or to enjoy the pleasures of sin in this world ruled by the usurper Satan? Suppose God chose not to promise us any "perks" for becoming a Christian? Would we choose Christ anyway, simply because we loved him?

....

The answer that Ittai gave to David rings down through the years as one of the finest affirmations of loyalty in human history. "I vow by God and by your own life that wherever you go, I will go, no matter what happens—*whether it means life or death.*"

How humbled and thrilled David must have felt at this statement of true friendship from a Philistine while his own son had turned against him! In fact, later when David organized the remnants of his army, he divided it into thirds, commanded by Joab and Abishai, his nephews who had served with him from the beginning, and Ittai the Philistine, who had served with him a few days.

....

Loyalty like Ittai's can truly be trusted. He is not going to desert you for a better offer. He is not going to want his contract renegotiated. You can count on him to the death. Can anyone count on us? Can God?

....

How Ittai and David met is a matter of conjecture, so we will not dwell on it here except to say that since Ittai was exiled from Philistine land and came immediately to David, it seems to indicate a prior friendship dating from years before when David had spent time in Gath. Apparently during the intervening years, Ittai had become such a strong promoter of David that his countrymen got sick of it, accused him of treason, and booted him out into exile with his six hundred converts to "Davidism."

....

Does anyone know who our King is, or are we the silent type when it comes to witnessing for Christ? God is looking for people like Ittai. Can he find them in us?

....

20 The Intrepid Trio
Part 1

1 SAMUEL 11:1-2; 2 SAMUEL 10:1-5; 17:27-29;
1 CHRONICLES 19:1-5

Shobi, Machir, and Barzillai were a team. They knew how to work together, though they were very different. Different in age, in race, in background, in wealth, and in abilities, yet one in purpose. They banded together to make provisions available for David and the two thousand-plus people who had to pack up and leave Jerusalem in only twenty-four hours to go into exile. With no time to prepare necessities of life for more than a day or two, David's followers found themselves in need. But not for long because down the road into Mahanaim came the intrepid trio with their porters and animals, bringing bedding, bowls, clay pots, wheat, barley, flour, roasted grain, beans, lentils, honey, curds, sheep, and cheese—all for David and his entourage!

Please notice that all this (enough for more than two thousand people!) was given freely with no expectation of payment or return. Nobody knew at this time what would happen with David, so who knew if he would ever be able to repay them? No, all these things were donations, pure and simple.

....

How willing are we to share what God has given us with our fellow Christians who are in need? True sharing does not expect repayment—ever!

....

Each of these men is interesting in his own right as well as in his teamwork. Let us consider each one separately.

Shobi was a nonroyal son of Nahash, the king of the Ammonites, who were perennial enemies of Israel. Once, when Saul was king of Israel, Shobi's father had threatened to poke out the right eyes of all the men from the Jabesh-gilead area as their payment to him for sparing their lives. That man was nasty! Saul defeated him in battle, but Nahash never forgot that humiliation because later, when David was a fugitive from Saul, Nahash apparently aided David in his attempts to avoid death at Saul's hands.

When Nahash died, his royal son Hanun succeeded the throne. He was as nasty as his father had been. When David sent a delegation to congratulate him on his new job as king, Hanun shaved off half of their beards, cut off their clothes at the waist, and sent them home in disgrace. Nasty! Like father, like son.

Now Shobi had a choice. He could follow in the footsteps of his father and brother, or he could chart a new course for himself. He chose the latter, so we see him lending his organizational skills to supply David and his followers in exile.

....

It is popular these days to blame our families, our neighborhood, or our society for how badly we turn out. "It's not my fault," we say. "What did you expect, considering the environment I grew up in?" Shobi shows us that, despite a bad environment, we can choose to do right—that we ourselves are accountable to God for our own actions and choices.

....

21 The Intrepid Trio
Part 2

2 SAMUEL 9:4-5; 19:31-40; 1 KINGS 2:7

Let us continue with the last two members of the intrepid trio, Machir and Barzillai.

Machir ("salesman"), son of Ammiel ("a devoted ally"), from Lo-debar ("place of no pasture"), is only mentioned twice in Scripture, but both times he is doing the same thing. He provided for the helpless Mephibosheth before David adopted him as his son, and here Machir is one of the team providing for a destitute David. In neither case could Machir hope for any return on his investment, yet he gladly did what he could to help. I think he was the one of the three who concocted the idea to help David and then enlisted the aid of the others since the task was larger than his resources could handle. The man just loved to help people!

....

Lots of people need all sorts of help these days. The continual lockout of God from our society has set many people adrift. They need help. Are we among those gifts to the local church listed as "helps" in 1 Corinthians 12:28?

....

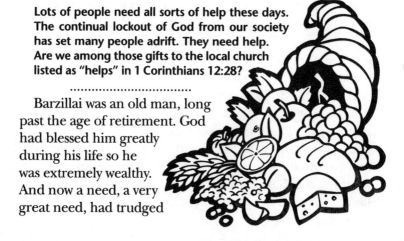

Barzillai was an old man, long past the age of retirement. God had blessed him greatly during his life so he was extremely wealthy. And now a need, a very great need, had trudged wearily into his backyard since his home in Rogelim was only a short distance from Mahanaim, where David and his followers had collapsed. He could meet that need. He had plenty and some to spare. So, teaming up with Shobi and Machir, he became the principal source of the needed provisions.

....

Has God blessed us with material things? Why do we think he has done that? So that we can spend it all on ourselves? Could it be that he wants us to use what he has provided for the material needs of other believers?

....

Later, when David did return to his throne, he offered Barzillai a blank check as it were. "Come live with me at the palace, and I will take care of you for the rest of your life," he said.

Barzillai refused, saying he did not want to be a burden to David but would rather live out his life in the familiar surroundings of Rogelim. He was ready to help when needed, but he would not presume upon the kindness of others simply because it was offered.

....

There are many in our society today who will take unfair advantage of any offer of help, even to the point of cheating, lying, and biting the hand that feeds them. May God keep us from misbehaving like that.

....

However, Barzillai did not force others to abide by his principles. His son Chimham did go with David, and apparently, some time later, left David's welfare list and went into business for himself as an innkeeper. The inn was still called by his name several hundred years later.

David never forgot Barzillai's kindness. On his deathbed, he instructed his son Solomon to always make sure that Barzillai's family was taken care of.

The last mention of this grand old man is most interesting. Hundreds of years later, a priest who was returning to Israel from Babylon had lost his genealogy. However, he had married a descendant of Barzillai's. So what did he do? He took the name of his wife's ancestor as his own and became known as Barzillai (see Ezra 2:61)!

....

We will be remembered with admiration and respect if, like Barzillai, we are people of principle and honesty. Others will be glad to be associated with us! There they are—Shobi, Machir, and Barzillai. Have they gained our admiration? Do we emulate their qualities of kindness, generosity, and unselfishness?

....

22 Power, Prophecy, and Paralysis

1 KINGS 13:1-32; 2 KINGS 23:15-18

There they were! Just as he had been told! The lion and the donkey standing next to each other, and lying before them in the road was the body of the man of God from Judah. The old man recognized him right away as the man who earlier had sat at his table "talking shop." The lion had not mauled him, nor had the lion touched the donkey! What's more, the donkey seemed unafraid of the lion!

As the old man approached, very cautiously I might add, the lion turned its head, looked at him, and walked off into the woods. The old man loaded the body of the man of God onto the donkey, took him back, and buried him in the grave where the old man would one day be buried himself. . . . But we are ahead of ourselves. What led up to this strange scenario?

King Jeroboam stood before the golden calf he had erected in Bethel on the southern border of his new kingdom of Israel. He was offering sacrifices to it to show his subjects that they no longer needed to travel down to Solomon's brand-new temple in Jerusalem to worship. They now had their own gods.

....

We should be forewarned that when anyone offers us short-cuts in the worship of God, they will probably lead us astray.

....

Suddenly, there was a stir in the crowd of onlookers. A man pushed through and approached Jeroboam. He was a man of God sent from Judah with a message for the king: "O altar, the Lord says that a child named Josiah shall be born into the family line of David, and he shall sacrifice upon you the priests from the shrines on the hills who come here to burn incense; and men's bones shall be burned upon you. This altar will split apart, and the ashes on it will spill to the ground."

King Jeroboam was furious! Pointing at the man of God, he shouted, "Arrest that man!"

Immediately the king's arm froze, and he could not pull it down. At the same moment, his altar split apart and the ashes poured out! Jeroboam knew he was surrounded by the power of the God whom he had rejected. So he ate humble pie and begged the man of God to appeal to God to heal his arm. He did not want to spend the rest of his life with his arm in so peculiar a position!

....

Setting ourselves against God is a very foolish thing to do. Although most likely nothing as dramatic as what happened to Jeroboam will happen to us, we might eventually find that God will use the very thing with which we have opposed him to humble us and cause us to recognize his power.

....

God graciously healed Jeroboam's arm, and in an effort to regain his lost dignity, Jeroboam offered reward and refreshment to the man of God. He answered, "The Lord has given me strict orders not to eat anything or drink any water while I'm here." And off he went toward home.

The news of what happened traveled fast. An old man who had once been a prophet lived in Bethel. When he heard that an active prophet was in the area, he hurried out to see if he could find him. He found the man of God from Judah taking a break under a tree.

"Are you the man of God from Judah?" the old prophet asked.

"I am."

"Come home with me for a meal. I'd love to chat with you about your work."

"Sorry, I can't. God told me not to hang around here in Israel."

"Well, I am a prophet too. An angel of God just told me to bring you back to my home. Come on."

So the man of God went back to the old man's house.

....

We need to be very cautious when people, even Christian people, tell us that they have received a special revelation from God with a message for us. We need to check it out by the Word of God (Isa. 8:19-20). If it agrees with God's Word, then it is not a special revelation; it has already been revealed. If it does not agree with God's Word, then it might be a revelation, but it is definitely not from God. God never contradicts himself.

....

While they were talking, the old man really did receive a message from God for the man of God from Judah. "The Lord says that because you have been disobedient . . . your body shall not be buried in the grave of your fathers."

You know the rest of the story since we began with it. But maybe these questions are still rattling around in your mind. Why didn't the lion eat the carcass? Why didn't the lion harm the donkey? Why wasn't the donkey afraid of the lion? The Bible does not answer these questions, but here is my theory. See what you think of it. The lion represents Satan. The donkey represents a servant of God. The lion was allowed to carry out God's punishment on the man of God, but no more than that. The lion was under the control of God; Satan is under the control of God. He can do only what God allows. God did not allow the lion to kill the donkey. The donkey was not afraid of the lion. The servant of God need not fear Satan because "greater is he that is in you, than he that is in the world" (1 John 4:4, KJV).

23 Performance under Pressure

1 Kings 17:1; 18:1-16; James 5:17

Obadiah was badly frightened. He was basically a timid soul who preferred anonymity to fame. He worshiped the Lord, but he worked for the two worst bosses you could imagine: the cruel and vindictive Queen Jezebel and her unpredictable and wicked husband, King Ahab. Obadiah had probably inherited his job of palace overseer from his father since positions like his were often passed down from father to son.

As Obadiah thought of what he was doing secretly (on his own time, and with his own resources, I think), he shivered with fear. If Jezebel ever found out, she would kill him as she had already killed many of God's young prophets-in-training. Obadiah had just returned from the two caves where he was keeping one hundred prophets of God alive with bread and *water* during an intense drought that had lasted for three and a half years! What resourcefulness and organization it had required. What tremendous stress Obadiah had endured week after week as he consistently had done what he felt God wanted him to do *under the very noses of Ahab and Jezebel!*

·····································

Are we willing to get involved in service to others at the cost of our own comfort and peace of mind? Are we willing to do

what's right even when we are truly afraid? Are we willing to use our skills and resources to serve the Lord?

....

And now Ahab had summoned Obadiah to appear before him immediately. As he stumbled toward the king's quarters, all sorts of dreadful pictures flashed through his mind.

"Obadiah, you and I are going out to search the land for grass for my horses. Be ready to travel in an hour."

Relief flooded Obadiah's heart. *I'm not going to be executed! At least, not this time!*

....

Imagine a king who was more interested in grass for his horses than in food for his starving people! And yet, do others see us focusing on our own material possessions rather than on the needs of those for whom God has given us some responsibility and accountability?

....

Off they went, and after arranging a meeting time and place, they separated to search in opposite directions. It was a rather hopeless task. No rain or dew had fallen for three and a half years. Brooks had dried up, the sky was yellow with dust, and the earth was like iron (Deut. 28:23-24).

Obadiah wandered around, hardly knowing what direction to take. Suddenly he looked up and there was Elijah the prophet! Could it really be? Ever since Elijah had predicted its coming, Ahab had been blaming him for the drought. Ahab had turned the whole Middle East upside down trying to locate him, and now here he was!

....

Have we ever been guilty of blaming others for the bad results of what we know to be our own sins?

....

As Obadiah stared in disbelief, Elijah said, "Go tell Ahab that I am here."

Poor Obadiah! Listen, as three and a half years of pent-up tension, stress, and fear poured out of his heart into what he hoped was Elijah's sympathetic ear: "What harm have I done to you that you are sending me to my death? For I swear by God that the king has searched every nation and kingdom on earth from end to end to find you. And each time when he was told 'Elijah isn't here,' King Ahab forced the king of that nation to swear to the truth of his claim. And now you say, 'Go and tell him Elijah is here'! But as soon as I leave you, the Spirit of the Lord will carry you away, who knows where, and when Ahab comes and can't find you, he will kill me; yet I have been a true servant of the Lord all my life. Has no one told you about the time when Queen Jezebel was trying to kill the Lord's prophets, and I hid a hundred of them in two caves and fed them with bread and water? And now you say, 'Go tell the king that Elijah is here'! Sir, if I do that, I'm dead!"

Elijah assured Obadiah that he wouldn't disappear. Obadiah obeyed Elijah's directive and then disappears himself from the pages of Scripture.

....

But what a lesson he has taught us! Put God first and trust in his all-powerful care (even if you are afraid!).

....

24 My Man Micaiah
Part 1

1 KINGS 22:1-9; 2 CHRONICLES 18:1-8

Life had become bor-r-r-ing! No battles had burst out for three years, and King Ahab was antsy.

....

Wicked people like Ahab are uncomfortable with peace and quiet. Isaiah 57:20-21 says, "But those who still reject me are like the restless sea, which is never still, but always churns up mire and dirt. There is no peace, says my God, for them!" Are we more comfortable when the radio or TV is constantly on? Do we like our music loud—the louder, the better? Do we live for the weekend parties? Then, maybe you know how Ahab was feeling. We can try some quiet once in a while or a quiet weekend at home; the noise of our everyday lives can overpower God's voice.

....

So Ahab developed a plan that would involve King Jehoshaphat of Judah, who was coming for a state visit. Ahab saw Jehoshaphat (we'll call him "Josh" from now on) as a kind, agreeable man, just the type who could be used. Therefore, when Josh arrived, Ahab asked him, "Will you send your army with mine to recover Ramoth-gilead?" (Ramoth-gilead was an important Israelite city that had been captured by Syria years before.)

Josh's answer was the expected one: "Of course! You and I are brothers; my people are yours to command." But then Josh added something else: "We should ask the Lord first, to be sure of what he wants us to do."

....

Are you a believer in the Lord as Josh was? God wants you to be kind and helpful to others. But you need to make sure first that you are not aiding an unbeliever in his sin. Josh made the mistake of promising to help first before trying to discover God's will for him. You must serve God first and others second. Then if others take advantage of you, you know God is allowing it for his purposes.

....

Ahab was ready. He had four hundred false prophets waiting for just such an occasion as this. These prophets were employed by Ahab's wife, Jezebel, in her degraded worship of the Sidonian Baal, a false god. Ahab called them in and asked them, "Shall I attack Ramoth-gilead, or not?"

Now these prophets didn't worry about telling the truth because they were false prophets of a false god. But they did worry about saving their necks because Jezebel was not a pleasant boss to work for. She had already killed prophets who had disagreed with her, so there was no question in their minds about what they had to say!

"Yes, go ahead, for God will help you conquer it," they all cried in unison. While his prophets chanted on and on, I'm sure Ahab watched Josh's face closely, hoping to see satisfaction settling there. But what he saw and heard dashed his hopes.

Josh asked, "Isn't there a prophet of the Lord here? I'd like to ask him, too."

....

It is interesting that the more of God's truth we know from reading and studying God's Word, the less we can be fooled by Satan's counterfeits. Because Josh knew God, he realized that these prophets were not telling God's truth; they were repeating Ahab's wishes. Would we have been fooled by these prophets, or do we know enough of God and his Word to recognize lies?

....

Well, Ahab badly needed Josh's help, and Josh was being difficult, and all of Ahab's plans were falling to pieces, and oh, well—maybe, just maybe, this time it would be different—so . . .

Ahab mumbled, "Well, there's one, but I hate him, for he never prophesies anything good. He always has something gloomy to say. His name is Micaiah, the son of Imlah."

....

Poor Ahab! When we choose to reject God and live a life given over to evil as he did, we will live in constant fear of the truth because it will always focus on our sins. If we are doing what God wants of us, the truth will be welcome, not dreaded and feared.

....

There must have been an embarrassed silence before Josh said, "Oh, come now! Don't talk like that!"

More silence while Ahab waited for Josh to say it wasn't necessary to call in Micaiah, but Josh was waiting too. Finally, probably heaving a huge sigh, Ahab called for an officer and commanded him to hunt Micaiah down and conduct him into the royal court as soon as possible.

25 My Man Micaiah
Part 2

1 KINGS 22:10-14; 2 CHRONICLES 18:9-13

While the officer was out looking for Micaiah, Ahab and Josh went to the open area by the gate of Samaria to be seen together since Josh's visit was an official one. They sat on thrones (were they portable?) and were dressed in their royal robes.

Before them the four hundred false prophets were going on at a great rate, trying to convince the two kings that they really would win the battle against Ramoth-gilead if they went. In order to make his "prophecy" more dramatic, Zedekiah, the spokesman for the chanting prophets, produced some iron horns shaped like oxen's horns and, holding them up on his head, started dancing around, shouting, "You shall gore the Syrians with these until they are destroyed!"

The rest of the four hundred kept on chanting, "Go ahead and attack Ramoth-gilead, for the Lord will cause you to triumph!"

....

It must have been quite a show! But shows like this are only needed when the truth is missing and the falseness needs to be dramatized in order to be believed. Many television commercials operate on this same principle used by Zedekiah and his four hundred men. Jesus also warns against using this kind of constant repetition when we try to convince God to answer

our prayers the way we want him to. In Matthew 6:7-8, he
says, "Don't recite the same prayer over and over as the
heathen do, who think prayers are answered only by repeating them again and again."

....

Meanwhile, what was happening with the officer sent
to find Micaiah? It must have taken a while, but when he
found the prophet, the officer told him what the king had
ordered, and then he added a comment of his own. "Now
listen, all the other prophets are encouraging the king.
Please let your word be like theirs, and speak encouragement." In other words, the officer was saying something
like this: "Micaiah, just for once, can't you be agreeable?
You always cause trouble when you prophesy against King
Ahab. He gets upset, Jezebel gets upset, and the whole
royal court gets into an uproar! Can't you be a nice fellow
and fix the truth a little so that you will be more in line
with what the majority is saying? Please?!"

....

At this point let me ask you what you would do if you were
Micaiah. Would you change the truth so as not to offend
others? Have you ever done that? Or would you enjoy your
role as a "nasty" prophet and pronounce your troublesome
prophecy with great satisfaction? Let's see what Micaiah did.

....

First (and this is the key to Micaiah's whole life and
should be the key to yours as well), he told the officer,
"This I vow, that I will say only what the Lord tells me to!" No
compromise there! The truth, the whole truth, and nothing but the truth! And because this was Micaiah's life
principle, he was free—truly free—of the fear of man.
He knew that he belonged to God, that God's truth came
first, and that he could count on God's perfect will in any
fallout from the stand he had taken.

....

Have we ever found ourselves unable to stand for the truth
because we were afraid of what our friends might think?
Maybe we need to take a second look at who our friends are.
Would Jesus consider them his friends? Do we, like Micaiah,
trust God with the results of our taking a stand for him?

....

My Man Micaiah, Part 2

Second, Micaiah delivered the message to Ahab and
Josh that God had given him. The results were not what
the average man would consider pleasant, but I think that
Micaiah didn't mind them at all because he knew that
God loved him and that he was doing what pleased God.

"But what was the message for Ahab? What were those
results?" you ask. Stay tuned.

26 **My Man Micaiah** *Part 3*

1 KINGS 22:15-40; 2 CHRONICLES 18:14-34

hen Micaiah reached the gate of Samaria, he saw the show being staged by the four hundred false prophets for the benefit of the two kings. There was Zedekiah dancing around with his horns, and there were the chanting prophets. How funny they must have looked to Micaiah! All that trouble to try to turn falsehood into truth! So when Ahab saw Micaiah and beckoned him to the front, Micaiah just couldn't resist having a little fun. He might even force Ahab to demand the truth.

Here came Ahab's question: "Micaiah, shall we attack Ramoth-gilead, or not?"

"Go ahead and attack Ramoth-gilead, for the Lord will cause you to triumph!" Micaiah responded.

What? Micaiah, have you caved in to the pressure to be like everyone else? Wait and see.

Ahab then spoke, "How many times must I tell you to speak only what the Lord tells you to?"

What is going on here? Ahab asking for the truth? Ahab implying that what Micaiah had just said (and what the four hundred prophets had been chanting for so long) was not the truth? What could have caused Ahab to get himself into such a predicament as this?

You know the answer, don't you! Micaiah had mimicked the four hundred prophets in tone, rhythm, facial expression, body language, and words, so that everyone there knew he was having some fun at their expense. It was obvious that he was joking. So King Ahab, in order to preserve his dignity, had to ask for the truth.

Micaiah quickly obliged. "I saw all Israel scattered upon the mountains as sheep without a shepherd. And the Lord said, 'Their king is dead; send them to their homes,'" Micaiah stated solemnly. No humor this time, only seriousness and sadness.

"Didn't I tell you he would not prophesy good concerning me, but evil!" shouted Ahab at Josh.

Micaiah cut in. "I'm not finished yet," and he went on to tell about a most unusual vision he had seen, a vision that is very difficult to fully understand. In it God seemed to give permission to a lying spirit to influence the four hundred prophets to encourage Ahab to go to his death at Ramoth-gilead as God's judgment on him for his sinful life.

....

You need to remember that you can never fully understand an all-powerful, all-knowing God with your finite mind. The Bible makes it clear that God controls all that happens, and if you don't understand exactly how it all works, you need to humbly accept what is clear, and leave the uncertainties with him.

....

Anyway, Zedekiah was furious because Micaiah had suggested that he was a liar. He slapped Micaiah across the face and shouted that it was Micaiah who was the liar.

Micaiah's calm response was, "You will see for yourself who is lying when you are hiding out after the battle is lost."

Ahab had Micaiah arrested and thrown into prison to be fed with bread and water until Ahab returned in peace from the battle.

Micaiah's comment about that was, "If you return in peace, it will prove that the Lord has not spoken through me. Take note of what I've said," Micaiah called to the crowd watching this spectacle.

73

Do you see what Micaiah was facing? He would either be in prison for the rest of his life, or he would be proven to be a false prophet and be discredited for the rest of his life. Some choice for being true to God, isn't it? But you know, somehow I can't imagine Micaiah getting bitter and angry and moping about in prison. Instead, I see him singing songs of praise and glory to God, being a witness for God, and thoroughly enjoying a relationship with God that freed his soul, even though his body might be shackled in a dungeon.

We are never told what eventually happened to Micaiah, but it doesn't really matter. Whatever it was, we know that today he is in heaven, delighting in the presence of his Lord.

Ahab thought he could outsmart God, probably because Josh, a believer in God, was so easy to con. Ahab's plan was to go into battle disguised as a common soldier while Josh would go dressed as a king; thus God wouldn't know where Ahab was and therefore couldn't cause him to die. Such foolish thinking!

What happened to Ahab? He was hanging out in a part of the battle where there was not much action. A bored Syrian soldier decided to kill time by shooting arrows. He shot an aimless arrow into the air, and God directed that arrow through the waist joint in Ahab's armor. That same evening Ahab died just as God had said through Micaiah.

....

Sin tends to muddy your thinking about God's character and power and makes him much smaller in your mind than he really is. There is no way we can fool or beat God. It reminds me of the title of a Broadway play: *Your Arm's Too Short to Box with God.* **As you examine your life, who are you more like, Micaiah or Ahab? Ask God to help you with those "Ahab areas" in your life, and thank him for his help with the "Micaiah modifications" as well.**

....

27 Poverty, Pots, and Provision

2 Kings 4:1-7

I suppose I could say she was poor: a widow, no money, only a little olive oil in a jar, in debt, and with a cruel creditor breathing down her neck and threatening to take her two sons as slaves instead of payment! A hopeless picture, wouldn't you say?

But, I could also say that she was rich: in faith, in friends, and in that special brand of fortitude to do anything necessary to protect her children!

She came to the prophet Elisha one day and apprised him of her predicament. She told him about her godly husband, his death, her debt, the threat to her boys, and her destitution.

....

Her faith in her husband's God would not let her turn away from him as so many do in bitterness when they find themselves in dire straits. Do we shake our fists in God's face when things are not going well or, like the widow, stretch out our hands to him and ask for his help?

....

When he asked her what she had for starters, she replied, "Nothing at all, except a jar of olive oil."

I wonder how we would react if we were to hear the instructions she received from Elisha. "Borrow every container you can from your friends and neighbors, take them all home, shut the door, and you and your sons work together at filling all those containers with oil from your jar." First, she would have to humiliate herself because her borrowing would signal her poverty to everyone! Next, she would probably have to explain her reasons for the borrowing to incredulous friends and neighbors!

"You don't mean to tell me you actually believe you will be able to fill all those pots from your one little jar of oil?" "You must be bonkers!" "You sure you aren't just having a garage sale, where you'll sell my pot and keep the money?" "How much income do you expect to get from that crazy scheme? It will never be enough!" Etc., etc.

Third, she and her sons had to work hard to carry out their responsibility in the whole setup. She could not just sit back and wait for her relief to be doled out to her by some government agency.

·····

Does our pride get in the way of doing whatever we can to help care for our own needs? Is our faith in God's power sufficient to overcome the mocking unbelief of this world's naturalistic thinkers? Do we believe that God can meet our needs in spite of all appearances to the contrary? If so, then we truly are living by faith.

·····

The widow and her sons set to work, begging, cajoling, pleading, collecting, carrying, arranging, pouring, replacing, until every last container was filled to the brim with olive oil! Only then did the miraculous oil stop flowing! The story seems to suggest that the amount of oil available was determined by the number of containers. If there had been more containers, there would have been more oil! Fewer containers, less oil!

·····

Oil is often a symbol of the Holy Spirit in Scripture. He will fill every area of ourselves that we make available to him! We should therefore strive to provide many "pots" in our lives for his Spirit to fill.

·····

Was the oil sufficient for her needs? She sold it all (it must have been high quality oil!), paid off her debt, and had enough income remaining to provide for herself and her sons! Her diligence was handsomely rewarded!

....

Spiritual diligence will also be handsomely rewarded in increased faith, resources, power against spiritual enemies, and ability to provide for the spiritual needs of our friends in Christ, to say nothing of the joy at seeing God's power at work in our lives.

....

28 The Captivating Captive

2 KINGS 5:1-19

She lived in Syria, but it was not her home. She was captured by Syrians, but not by bitterness. She served a Syrian, but not Satan. She supplied the information that changed a Syrian's outlook, but not her own. She is unnamed to us, but not to God.

One of the most charming cameo appearances in the drama of Scripture is an extra with a bit part that is not a bit unimportant. Her selfless act shines its sunny rays from the saga of the sick Syrian general. But her story begins during the storms of violence that often threatened the borderland in which she had lived. Syrian raiders had ripped her away from her family, friends, and familiar surroundings and carried her captive to Damascus, where she had been sold to Mrs. Naaman as her slave.

Two of the things that tend to make us angry are unfairness and injustice when we perceive ourselves as the victims. We presume that we own rights that have been destroyed. If we claim Christ as our Master, we have turned over to him all our rights—we no longer have any. If he sees fit to allow "unfairness" and "injustice" in our lives, we should not get upset but, rather, expectantly look forward to what he is setting up for us.

You see, what happened to this little maid was a setup for Naaman's sake. He needed her desperately, and God arranged it. So when the news of his leprosy got around, there she was, possessing the information he needed most. She could have withheld it, figuring to get her revenge for all the trouble he had caused her. But she was no slave to anger, bitterness, or revenge. She had committed her rights to God, and he had placed her where what she knew could accomplish God's perfect purpose and will. So she spoke her knowledge.

....

God has entrusted us with the knowledge of how the leprosy of sin can be cured. He has allowed us to continue living in an alien world so that we can dispense the information we have. Are we doing so, or are we keeping quiet?

....

She was believed! A little slave girl's simple statement set in motion the machinery of two national governments. I wonder why Mr. and Mrs. Naaman put so much trust in her information? She must have been an honest and hard worker, gaining a good reputation with her masters.

Her information was not exactly correct; it was not Elisha who would heal her master. But it was close enough, and God used it. Naaman went to Elisha, who sent a message that instructed Naaman to wash in the Jordan. He did and was cured! This little slave girl's message led to the healing and conversion of an enemy general.

....

Never refuse to witness for fear that it will not be good enough. God can use any witness that is given with love and concern for those who are dying in sin.

....

What a gal! Do you know of anyone in the Bible (other than our Lord Jesus himself) who illustrates love for one's enemies better than she? I don't!

29 "Pain" Prays; God Gives

1 CHRONICLES 4:9-10

······································

Have we ever come to a long genealogy in the Old Testament and skipped it, figuring that it is only a list of unpronounceable names, so why bother? If we have, we have probably missed the story of Jabez tucked in the middle of the longest list of genealogies in the whole Bible. First Chronicles 1–9 is one genealogy after another, but in 4:9-10 is the story of Jabez, only two verses long, but a nugget of great value nonetheless.

······································

Let us reproduce his whole story right here. "Jabez was more honorable than his brothers, and his mother called his name Jabez, saying, 'Because I bore him in pain.' And Jabez called on the God of Israel saying, 'Oh, that You would bless me indeed, and enlarge my territory, that Your hand would be with me, and that You would keep me from evil, that I may not cause pain!' So God granted him what he requested" (NKJV).

Notice these facts: (1) He was more honorable than his brothers. Why? (2) His mother named him Jabez (which means "pain") because she said, "I bore him in pain." Why was that? (3) Jabez called on the God of Israel. Wonderful! But again, why? In his prayer he asked God to bless him, expand his territory, be with him, keep him from evil, and help him not to be a pain to others. (Notice the play on his name in this last request.) (4) God granted his requests! Why would God do that?

Would you agree that this little story raises many questions?

How would you like to be named Pain? Back in Old Testament days names were most often given according to their meanings. We are even told that Jabez's mother chose that name for him specifically because it meant "pain." Now why would a mother purposely saddle her baby boy with such a name?

"Because I bore him in pain," she answers.

"Yes, but aren't all children born with pain?" we ask.

"Not like this pain!" she retorts.

What could have been so awful about Jabez's birth? We aren't told. Could it have been that he was born deformed in some way? Maybe he had not been positioned correctly in the birth canal, and his delivery had been unusually long and excruciatingly painful. Whatever the reason, little Pain probably had to grow up amid the taunts and vicious jokes flung at him by his brothers and childhood acquaintances. (We all know how cruel children can be!) Can you imagine what an inferiority complex Jabez must have borne as an adult!

....

Have we ever taken time to think seriously about the deep emotional wounds we cause to those we give mocking or insulting nicknames? Of course we only mean it in fun, but we are not the insulted and humiliated ones. Remember, God takes it personally when we mistreat his children (see Matt. 25:45).

....

Jabez—despite his difficulties—entrusted his life to God. He had found that, unlike others, God listened when he talked to him. Could it be that this faith in God was what made him "more honorable" than his brothers?

....

We read in 1 Corinthians 1:27-29 that "God has chosen the foolish . . . , weak . . . , base . . . , [and] despised . . . that no flesh should glory in His presence" (NKJV). Might these adjectives have applied to Jabez had he been around? The wise, mighty, and noble often think they are self-sufficient and do not need or want God's help. Are we willing to be counted in the "Jabez group"?

....

But notice that Jabez's requests were all self-directed. He wanted blessing, wealth, power, protection from God, and acceptance from others. Yet, wonder of wonders, God granted them all to him! Why did God choose to give these gifts to Jabez when, often, he does not choose to do the same for others? God has not given us the answer here in Jabez's story, but maybe reading the following verses will help:

Psalm 37:3-5 (how to receive answers to prayer)
2 Chronicles 7:14 (the necessary attitude for answered prayer)
Jeremiah 29:13 (the proper focus for answered prayer)
Mark 11:24 (the conditional promise of answered prayer)
James 5:16 (the way to pray)
1 John 3:22 (the groundwork for answered prayer)

I wonder how many of these requirements for answered prayer were a part of Jabez's life? How many of them are a part of ours?

30 Looking for Loopholes?

JEREMIAH 35:1-19

Jaazaniah ("Jazzy" for short) was deeply puzzled. As he made the rounds to gather his relatives together, he kept wondering, *What is this all about? Why would the great prophet Jeremiah order us to meet with him, and in the Temple, no less? What could we have done wrong? We have tried to be law-abiding citizens. We have even obeyed the special laws of our Rechabite clan. I wish I could figure this out!*

As his clansmen kept quizzing him, Jazzy had to keep saying, "I don't know; I really don't know. I just received this message with no explanation at all."

When the Rechabites approached the Temple, Jeremiah met them. He conducted them into an upstairs side room, where they were asked to sit on the floor. Cups and jugs of wine were placed before. It was hard to tell anything from Jeremiah's face, so they sat there looking at each other, scratching their heads in confusion.

Finally Jeremiah spoke. "Drink the wine," he commanded.

The Rechabites were stunned. They had never expected anything like this. If they had been confused before, they were dumbfounded now. They all looked to Jazzy, their chief, to see what he would say.

But before we go any further with our story, we need to back up for a minute. You see, Jeremiah didn't have a clue as to what this was all about either. God had simply told him to collect the Rechabites in a room in the Temple and tell them to drink wine. No explanation as to why had been given.

....

There is an important lesson for us here. Jeremiah, Jazzy, and the Rechabites had all obeyed orders from God without knowing why those orders had been given. Are we as ready to obey God's Word without always knowing all the reasons? Or do we want to know all the whys and wherefores before we follow God's instructions?

....

Anyway, as Jazzy began to speak, all eyes were on him.

"We will drink no wine," he began. "Our forefather Jonadab, many years ago, commanded us, 'You shall drink no wine, you nor your sons, forever. You shall not build a house, sow seed, plant a vineyard, nor have any of these; but all your days you shall dwell in tents, that you may live many days in the land where you are pilgrims.'" Jazzy continued, "Thus we have obeyed the voice of Jonadab our forefather in all that he charged us." The meaning was clear. There would be no drinking of wine, now or ever, for the Rechabites.

If some of us had been there, we might have interrupted and said, "But, Jazzy, here's your chance! The great prophet of God, Jeremiah, has given you a golden opportunity to disobey the rules without being disobedient! Look, you are in this holy place, in God's very presence. God's prophet has told you to drink wine. What a loophole! Finally you can get out from under that outdated restriction, and nobody can fault you! Don't blow this opportunity, Jazzy! Drink the wine! Go ahead! Drink it!"

....

How do we feel about obeying God's Word? Are we constantly trying to find loopholes that allow us to get away with less than wholehearted obedience? Are we irritated at having to bow to God's authority? What an example the Rechabites should be to us.

And by the way, if we think this story teaches that a Christian cannot do this, that, or the other thing, we've missed

the point. Jonadab's rules were not necessarily good ones. The point is that obedience to authority is a lifestyle that pleases God. We should be looking to obey God even when it seems that disobedience will go unpunished.

What if the Rechabites had drunk the wine? They would have spoiled God's object lesson to Judah. Have we ever thought that God might want to use us as object lessons, too, but he can't trust us as he trusted the Rechabites?

....

And Jazzy might have answered us, "But you don't understand. We Rechabites are not looking for loopholes so we can disobey our forefather's rules and regulations. We delight in keeping them. We may not understand exactly why he gave them to us, but voluntary obedience gives us joy and peace and is its own reward. Good-bye, friends."

Jeremiah watched the Rechabites file out, and then God spoke again to him. God explained that the Rechabites were his object lesson to the nation of Judah. You see, God knew the Rechabites would continue to obey their forefather's commands. But God's people kept disobeying the commands of their heavenly Father. Which father was more deserving of obedience, Jonadab or God? Which father's authority was greater, Jonadab's or God's? Which father's commands were the better ones for people to obey, Jonadab's or God's? Yet which father was being obeyed, Jonadab or God?

....

Wouldn't we like our friends and family members to become believers in the Lord Jesus Christ? If we show them a life of consistent obedience to God, it is likely that they, too, will come to know God and submit to his authority and not become loophole seekers.

....

What eventually happened to them? Just listen to this! God said that because of their obedience and faithfulness to what they thought was right, there would always be a Rechabite throughout the rest of history standing in God's presence! What a reward!

31 How to Be Unpopular

JEREMIAH 36:1-32; 43:1-6; 45:1-5

As Baruch took the opportunity at a pause in Jeremiah's dictation to look at him, his heart almost broke. Poor Jeremiah! The stress, sorrow, and strain of his prophetic ministry had taken its toll. Shoulders bent, hair and face streaked with gray, eyes glistening with tears, Jeremiah resumed dictating, and Baruch resumed his careful transcription of the scathing words against Judah coming slowly through Jeremiah's lips from the Lord. How much Jeremiah loved his people, and how hard it was to have to be pronouncing such awful judgments upon them! How deeply Baruch respected and loved Jeremiah, and how hard it was to see him suffering so!

As the two men continued working, day after day, hour after hour, line by painstaking line, the bond between them strengthened and solidified. Baruch would do anything for Jeremiah, and Jeremiah valued and completely trusted his friend and secretary.

....

When God allows faithful children of his to experience suffering together, it is a blessing. James tells us to be happy when our lives are full of difficulties and temptations, for "when the way is rough, your patience has a chance to grow.

So let it grow, and don't try to squirm out of your problems. For when your patience is finally in full bloom, then you will be ready for anything, strong in character, full and complete" (James 1:3-4).

....

Finally the day came when Baruch laid down his quill. It was finished. At last! As he tenderly rolled up the scroll, he thought of how much of himself had gone into it, the tension of absolute accuracy, and the pressure of perfection. After all, they were God's very words that he had written! He felt as though he had gone through the labors of childbirth to bring forth this scroll, the most important thing he would ever do!

....

Is God's Word precious to us, or can we take it or leave it? I wonder, if we were to take pen in hand and write our own copy, or at least parts of it (and not be able to purchase one in a store), as the kings of Israel were supposed to do (Deut. 17:18-20), whether we might appreciate more the wonder of being able to own such a treasure?

....

But we are all human. Baruch was too. Somewhere along the line, he found himself wondering if he had made the best choice in befriending Jeremiah when he might have used his skills in the king's court as his brother, Seraiah, was doing (see Jer. 32:12 and 51:59). By throwing in his lot with Jeremiah, Baruch was sharing in his unpopularity with no opportunities for advancement. Jeremiah was right, of course, and the king was wrong—but still . . .

Then Jeremiah told Baruch that he had received a message from God for Baruch himself: "Are you seeking great things for yourself? Don't do it! For though I will bring great evil upon all these people, I will protect you wherever you go, as your reward."

....

God understands our weaknesses. He rewards us for faithfulness to him in the midst of our troubles. If advancement is not to be our lot here on earth because we have chosen him, it will certainly be ours in heaven, where the rewards will be eternal!

....

One day Jeremiah said to Baruch, who was visiting him in the dungeon beneath the king's palace where he was imprisoned, "Read the scroll in the Temple on the next day of fasting. . . . Perhaps even yet they will turn from their evil ways and ask the Lord to forgive them."

Baruch did as he was told. As he finished the reading, he was summoned to read it again to the officials of King Jehoiakim's court. When they heard it, they realized that if the king heard about it, Jeremiah and Baruch could lose their lives. Yet if the officials didn't tell the king about it and he found out, they could lose their own lives. They advised Baruch and Jeremiah to go into hiding while they told the king.

King Jehoiakim commanded that the scroll be read to him. As he listened, he became so furious that he cut the scroll to pieces and threw the whole thing in the fire!

....

How would we feel if we were Jeremiah or Baruch and heard that our life's work had been destroyed? Bitter? Angry at God? Vengeful? Often what seems to us to be ruin and tragedy will be the foundation for even greater ministry for God and glory to him.

....

At God's command, back to work they went: Jeremiah redictating and Baruch rewriting all that was written in the first scroll. No computers, no backup disks, no stored memory—hard, painstaking work all over again! And when they were finished, settling back and taking a breather, God told Jeremiah that there would be additional information this time! So the book of Jeremiah as we know it today is longer than the first scroll. This book has also been miraculously preserved in spite of the animosity of mankind toward books like this that identify them as sinners and pronounce judgment upon them.

....

Who knows if Jeremiah and Baruch even thought that their work would last so long. While they might have thought that

their book would be read by a kingdom that would reject its message, it has endured for more than twenty-five hundred years and has been taken to heart by millions. The work we do today might not seem fruitful, but we never know what God plans! Let's not take our responsibilities lightly; the results of our work could be around for years.

....

32 All's Well That Ends Well

JEREMIAH 38:1-13; 39:15-18

J erry!" shouted Ebed-melech. "Can you hear me? I'm Ebed, come to get you out!"

"Ebed! Hurry! I'm sinking in the mud down here! And thanks!"

"Here, Jerry, some old rags. I'll drop them down. Put them under your armpits; then slip your arms through the loops in these two ropes you see coming down at you. I have thirty men here to haul you up. We'll have you out soon!"

And thus, Jeremiah the prophet, the lone voice in Jerusalem speaking God's truth, was rescued from an unused well by Ebed-melech, an Ethiopian official in King Zedekiah's court.

Other officials—Israelite officials—had wanted Jerry dead. They had accused him of treason against Judah because he had said that the only way to stay alive was to surrender to King Nebuchadnezzar of Babylon, who had been besieging Jerusalem for two years. They had been responsible for persuading the spineless King Zedekiah to turn Jerry over to them. They then had Jerry lowered into the old well that was now used as the dungeon in the prison where he was already being held, hoping that he would die a slow death in the sucking mud at the bottom.

....

God's Word is often very unpopular with people because it tells them that surrender is the way to eternal life—surrender of person, pride, plans, and prospects to God. Therefore, faithful communicators of God's Word become unpopular as well. Jeremiah told it like it was. Our goal should be to do the same, whatever the consequences.

....

However, Jerry's enemies did not count on Ebed. His differences in nationality, skin color, and outlook were probably contributing factors in their discounting of him. But here was a man, a real man, ready to do what was right and be a "friend in deed," even though he was endangering his own position in the palace and maybe even his life.

He went to King Zedekiah, told him of Jerry's predicament, and asked permission to save his life. Yes, the same king who had just allowed for Jerry's presence in the well is being asked to permit his removal from the well.

....

I cannot help but think that Ebed-melech's request had been bathed in prayer before he brought it up to the king. How else can we explain his belief that his request would be granted? All evidence seemed to show that the opposite would happen. I admire his willingness to go through channels rather than trying to circumvent them, which human wisdom would have advised. It shows his trust in the power of God. Are we as willing to trust God in the face of all evidence to the contrary?

....

And then there was the matter of the old rags. Even though time was of the essence, Ebed was caring and thoughtful enough to realize that the rough ropes would be extremely painful to Jerry's armpits because of his own weight and the added suction of the sticky mud. So Ebed rummaged in the basement under the treasury building, found the rags he knew were there, and used them as padding to prevent pain and rope burns as Jerry was being rescued.

....

Ebed was an official. Knowing the location of old rags is not usually considered part of an official's necessary knowledge. But Ebed did not consider such knowledge beneath him. He showed himself to be a loving, thoughtful, creative, humble servant of God and God's people. When people describe us, can they say similar things about us?

....

What was the eventual outcome? Jerusalem was overrun by Nebuchadnezzar. Jerry's enemies were killed. King Zedekiah was blinded and carried away into captivity. Jerry was left behind with the peasants and poor folk considered too worthless to deport or kill. And what of Ebed-melech? Listen to what God said to him! "I will do to this city everything I threatened; I will destroy it before your eyes, but I will deliver you. You shall not be killed by those you fear so much. As a reward for trusting me, I will preserve your life and keep you safe."

....

God delights to say to those who have put their trust in him, "I give them eternal life, and they shall never perish; neither shall anyone snatch them out of My hand" (John 10:28, NKJV). Have we entrusted our lives to Jesus and claimed this promise?

....

Hanging Out at the Temple Mall

LUKE 2:21-38

Day after day, there she was—the weird old lady, hanging out and talking to anybody who would listen. Anna was thought to be a religious nut by most of the money changers and merchants whose booths were scattered around the courtyards of Herod's Temple. They were in the business of getting rich off the pilgrims coming to the Temple to do their worship thing. But she seemed uninterested in financial reward, spending her time praying, fasting, and worshiping God. And oh, how she could talk! People in general tended to avoid her, but there were some few who listened carefully to her words since she had a reputation as a prophetess.

So she was there when it happened.

Then there was Simeon, another golden-ager that frequented the Temple as well. Most days there he was, a male counterpart to Anna: devoted to God, controlled by the Holy Spirit, and telling anyone who would listen that the Messiah would soon be there. He said that it had been revealed to him by

the Holy Spirit. On this particular day he, too, had
come to the Temple.

So he was there when it happened.

....

**Where and with whom do we hang out? We are often labeled
by the company we keep. Do we enjoy being with other
Christians, or do we find them boring? Our hangouts and
friends are excellent indicators of where we are spiritually.
When we are where non-Christians are, do we enjoy witnessing for Christ, or do we make excuses to ourselves as to why
we should not? We never know what great blessing from God
we might miss if we are not interested in his people or in
proclaiming him.**

....

It happened as a couple entered the temple, carrying
a forty-day-old baby boy. As they approached, Simeon,
prompted by the Holy Spirit, walked up and lifted the
baby from his mother's arms, snuggling him in his own.
As the respectful parents looked on wonderingly and with
a little apprehension, Simeon spoke.

"Lord, now I can die content! For I have seen him as
you promised me I would. I have seen the Savior you have
given to the world. He is the Light that will shine upon the
nations, and he will be the glory of your people Israel!"

Mary and Joseph looked at each other in amazement!
They knew that their baby Jesus was special, but how
did this old man know? As they turned back toward
him, his eyes mirrored sadness. Looking straight at
Mary, he spoke again.

"A sword shall pierce your soul," he said softly, "for this
child shall be rejected by many in Israel, and this to their
undoing. But he will be the greatest joy of many others."
They saw him smile gently as he said these words. Then he
finished with, "And the deepest thoughts of many hearts
shall be revealed."

He returned the baby to his parents, who turned to go.
But there, standing behind them, was Anna. She had been
listening to Simeon's words. A smile straight from her soul
brightened her wrinkled face as she began telling pass-
ersby that the Messiah had finally arrived! Intermingled

with thanksgivings and praises to God she continued her witness, unfazed by what others might think of her.

....

How serious are we about knowing God? Are we so in tune with him (like Simeon and Anna) that we can sense his presence in us and in other believers? Or do we just not hear or see God, even when he is speaking or doing something right in front of our noses? Time with God in prayer and time studying his revelations in the Bible will help us to keep our spiritual ears and eyes open.

....

34 Living on the Fringe

JOHN 1:43-48; 6:2-7; 12:20-22; 14:8-12; ACTS 1:13

Philip the disciple (hereafter known as Phil D.) just did not get it. Even though he had been the first to whom Jesus had said, "Follow me," he just did not seem to be able to follow closely. He was always there; he is still listed as being among the eleven disciples in Acts 1:13 after Jesus had returned to heaven, so he was always there. But he just never was close.

How can you make a judgment like that, you might ask? Well, read on.

When Phil D. went to find his friend Nathanael to tell him about Jesus, here is what Phil D. said: "We have found the Messiah!—the very person Moses and the prophets told about! His name is Jesus, the son of Joseph from Nazareth!" Now Moses and the prophets had written that the Messiah would be the son of a virgin with God as his Father. So when Phil D. called him "the son of Joseph," he indicated that his train of thought was focused on the physical rather than the spiritual nature of Jesus. And this focus continued in Phil D. as he is mentioned from time to time.

....

Which do we find it easier to dwell on, think about, sing about—our Lord Jesus Christ's deity or humanity? One indi-

cation of increasing maturity in our relationship with him is an ability to progress in our thoughts about him from how much he is human, like us, to how much he is divine, like his Father, God.

....

The five thousand men plus women and children had been listening to Jesus all day long. So had Phil D. and the rest of the disciples. When Jesus, testing him, asked Phil, "Where shall we buy bread to feed this crowd?" Phil D. failed the test. He did not say, "You can provide it, Lord." He did not even say, "We can't, but if anyone can, you can, Lord." No. Focused on the physical as usual, he said, "Eight months' wages would not be sufficient to buy enough bread for all these people." The situation was hopeless as far as he was concerned. He still did not understand Jesus' power.

....

In what direction do we look for the supply of our needs? Are we looking inward to ourselves, around to others, or up to God? Do we come up with Phil D.'s answers when faced with problems of supply and demand? Since it was God who created all that exists, we should learn to trust him to take care of us and our needs.

....

Remember the time when he needed Andrew's aid to bring some Greeks to Jesus? Phil D. had spent almost three years with Jesus and was still unsure whether he would welcome Gentile dogs into his presence. In all that time his understanding of Jesus was still distorted by personal considerations, personal prejudices.

....

The only way to become better acquainted with Jesus is to spend time with him, communicating through prayer and the study of God's Word. But even that will not be enough if we continue to live on the fringe, never willing to fully commit to his control, reserving for ourselves pet personal perspectives on life.

....

Finally Phil D. asked a question in the upper room during the time Jesus was spending with his disciples just before his arrest. Jesus had just claimed to be the way to his Father, and, in fact, that he himself was a perfect representation of the Father. So what does Phil D. ask?

"Lord, show us the Father and we will be satisfied."

Can you believe it? What had Jesus just said? Where were you, Phil D.?

"Have I been such a long time with you, Phil D., and still you do not know me?" Can you hear the sorrow in that question? "He who has seen me has seen the Father. How can you say, 'Show us the Father'?"

....

Does Phil sound a lot like us? You know, trusting in God yet sometimes struggling to really understand God's power and will. Notice that even though Phil just didn't seem to get it sometimes, he still trusted in Jesus and did not give up. In fact, according to tradition, Philip later became an evangelist in Turkey and was killed for his faith. We mustn't let slow starts ruin our faith or persistence in Christ. As we mature, we will understand more and possibly do great work for God. Philip never gave up, and neither should we.

....

35 A Different Kind of Roman

MATTHEW 8:5-13; LUKE 7:1-10

He was different, no question about it. Romans were not supposed to love the Jews. Jews were constantly instigating trouble for the Roman government with their religious hang-ups. They were the most difficult of all Rome's conquered peoples to handle. Yet, here he was, a Roman centurion headquartered in Capernaum, a hotbed of Jewish unrest, and he loved the Jews! He had even funded the building of a synagogue for them!

He was different, no question about it. The *Jews* loved *him!* Now that was an unbelievable fact! He was a Gentile dog! He was associated with the hated Roman army that had dominated them for too many years. Yet the Jews loved him and were willing to be his spokesmen to Jesus when he asked.

He was different, no question about it. He loved a servant of his who was at death's door. Normal Romans did not love servants, even healthy servants. After all, they were just servants, far below the social strata in which patrician Romans moved. And he was a centurion—a commander of one hundred elite Roman troops! Yet he loved his servant so much that he was devastated by the thought that this servant was dying!

> People respond positively to sincere thoughtfulness and kindness and to a heart of love concerned for others. Much unnecessary conflict and bloodshed would be avoided were these qualities present in us all. Can others detect them in us?

He was different, no question about it. Although in a position of unquestioned authority, accustomed to having men obey his every command, he was a totally humble man. He had heard of Jesus, the Galilean preacher and healer. His beloved servant desperately needed help. He wanted to ask for it, but knowing his own heart, he realized his own unworthiness. Besides, what might the Jewish Jesus think if a Roman approached him in person?

> Do we tend to think more highly of ourselves than we ought? It's easy to let ourselves believe that because we are class president or captain of the football team we are better than others. We should avoid the temptation, though, and see ourselves as the centurion saw himself—as someone who needs God.

He was different, no question about it. His kind of faith amazed even Jesus! When his Jewish emissaries approached Jesus with his request that Jesus heal his servant, Jesus said, "I will come and heal him." But as Jesus approached his home, the centurion hurriedly sent out some friends who intercepted Jesus with these words: "The centurion, our friend, said, 'Sir, don't inconvenience yourself by coming to my home, for I am not worthy of any such honor. . . . Just speak a word from where you are, and my servant boy will be healed! I know, because I am under the authority of my superior officers, and I have authority over my men. I only need to say "Go!" and they go; or "Come!" and they come; and to my slave, "Do this or that," and he does it.'"

His faith in Jesus' power and authority over disease, to

say nothing of distance, simply amazed Jesus. He had never seen such faith among the Jews, and he said so! In fact much to the Jews' chagrin, he continued, "Many Gentiles shall come from all over the world and sit down in the Kingdom of Heaven with Abraham, Isaac, and Jacob. And many an Israelite—those for whom the Kingdom was prepared—shall be cast out into outer darkness, into the place of weeping and torment."

Then he said to the centurion's friends, "What he has believed has happened." And when they returned to the house, they found the servant completely healed.

....

How big is our faith in Jesus Christ? Do we really believe that he can heal sin-sick souls? If we don't really believe he can, we might be missing out on some dramatic healing in our lives. Trust him and ask for his help.

....

36 How to Play Second Fiddle

MATTHEW 4:18; 10:2; MARK 1:16; 3:18; LUKE 6:14;
JOHN 1:40, 44; 6:8; 12:22; ACTS 1:13

I f you and I were living in New Testament times, something like this might occur:

"Hey, [your name], I want you to meet Andrew here."

"Andrew?" you ask.

"Yes, Andrew. You know, Andrew Bar-jona."

"Oh, hi, Andrew."

"[Your name], I am so glad to meet you," Andrew patiently greets you.

"You know Simon Bar-jona, don't you? Everyone calls him Peter—well, Andrew is his brother."

"Oh yes! Now I place you. I know all about your brother. He is always making news." And so on.

Andrew, you see, was always overshadowed by his more flamboyant, aggressive, outspoken, dynamic brother. Six of the eleven times Andrew is mentioned by name he is further identified as Simon Peter's brother. Every time both brothers are named, Andrew's name follows his brother's. Talk about playing second fiddle!

And when we realize that it was Andrew who followed Jesus first and introduced his brother to Jesus, it becomes even more remarkable that he was able to handle the second-fiddle position so well. And he did because he did not try to compete with Peter. Instead, he used his personality and quiet demeanor to serve his Lord in a wonderful way—*he kept bringing people to Jesus!*

....

How do we feel when others get all the glory? Are we willing to quietly serve our Lord, looking only for his "well done, good and faithful servant; enter into the joy of your Lord"?

....

Now you have to admit that when Andrew came home and said, "We have found the Messiah!" it was a pretty wild and unbelievable statement. For hundreds of years the Jews had been looking for their Messiah to come riding into Jerusalem as their King, deliver them from oppression, and set up his Kingdom on earth. And now, suddenly, a common fisherman comes home and says he has found the Messiah, as though the Messiah needed finding.

What nonsense! And yet the amazing thing is that Peter believed what his brother said, at least enough to allow him to bring him to Jesus! Why? Could it be that Andrew had established a reputation in his home for truthfulness, sincerity, and seriousness about the Scriptures so that his family had learned to pay attention when he spoke?

....

What kind of a reputation have we established in our families? Can we be believed when we speak? Will our relatives pay attention to our witness about Christ because our actions support our words? Or are we "phony baloneys" to them?

....

Then there was the time when all of Jesus' disciples were standing around looking at each other, wondering what to do. Jesus had just indicated that he was expecting them to provide enough food for a hungry crowd of five thousand men plus women and children. Philip had already said that even if they had the equivalent of eight months' wages (which they did not), it would not be sufficient to buy bread enough for everyone.

At this point, Andrew must have felt a tug on his robe.

He looked down, and there was a boy holding up a sack. "Here, mister. The Master can have my food if he wants."

And Andrew brought him to Jesus. Andrew was not stupid enough to think that the boy's offering was going to amount to anything, but he must have been impressed with the thought behind it and wanted his Lord to know about it.

You can imagine Andrew's shock as he was collecting the leftovers after the miraculous meal!

But my question is, Why did that boy choose to approach Andrew? He apparently was too shy to approach the Master himself, so he looked around at the Master's men. Peter was too busy organizing things; Matthew had his calculator out figuring the economics of it all; Thomas had that skeptical look on his face; James and John were too loud and "thunderous"; and then he saw Andrew—quiet, unassuming, kindly Andrew. The rest is history.

....

How approachable are we? Do we have time to listen, even to little children? Is there an aura about us that says, "I have time for you. I will not reject you. I care about you"?

....

Philip was worried. Andrew could see it as Philip approached him with several strangers in tow. He called Andrew aside.

"Andy, I don't know how to handle this. These guys are Greeks, and they want to see Jesus. What do I do? Remember when he sent us out and told us not to go to the Gentiles [Matt. 10:5] and when he himself said to that Canaanite woman that he was sent only to Israel [Matt. 15:24]. Should I even be talking to these 'dogs'?"

And Andrew answered, "Let's take them to Jesus and let him decide."

....

Do we ever try to do the Holy Spirit's work for him, choosing to whom we want to witness because we think they would make good Christians and choosing to whom we will not witness because we think they are the wrong sort of people? May God help us not to let our personal biases and prejudices get in the way of his work! As a witness, Andrew was

acceptable to his family, approachable to the boy, and adapt-able to the Greeks—three necessary characteristics of faith-ful witnesses. Can people see them in us?

....

Andrew—what a wonderful brother to have! I'm sure Peter deeply appreciated his brother, who brought him to Jesus!

37 The "Wow!" Life

JOHN 9:1-38

Blind! From birth! Bedraggled! Begging! What a life! Kicked out of the way, cursed at, mocked, ignored, persecuted—M. B. Blind sat by the road.

And now, overriding everything else, that question—that stupid, unthinking question he had just overheard: "Rabbi, why was this man born blind? Was it a result of his own sins or those of his parents?" Asked right out! As though he could not hear either! The cruel words sank deep into his heart.

Then the Rabbi spoke. "Neither. But to demonstrate the power of God."

Whew! M. B. thought. *That's better, at least the first part of what he said. But that last part—what does that mean?*

As M. B. listened with both ears, he was surprised to hear a spitting noise, then someone scraping around in the dust. Next he felt hands rubbing some sticky stuff on his eyes, and then he heard the voice of the Rabbi: "Go and wash in the Pool of Siloam."

....

Was there any medicinal value in the mud made from Jesus' spit and dust? If there was, why tell M. B. to wash it off? If there was not, why smear it on M. B.'s eyes at all? The whole procedure was ridiculous! Unless faith was being tested! When human wisdom says that something God wants us to do is

ridiculous, are we ready to place our faith in God or in the wisdom of men?

....

What was M. B. going to do? He did not know who this Rabbi was. If he followed the command and nothing happened, he would feel foolish and put upon. And yet, that sticky stuff on his eyes was drying hard and didn't feel wonderful. *I've got nothing to lose except my pride, and I don't have much of that anyway,* thought M. B., so off he went to Siloam's pool.

What happened? Faith was rewarded! M. B. gained his sight for the first time in his life! Imagine what it must have been like!

"Hey, mister, what is that over there?"

"You mean that tree?"

"Tree? Tree! So that's what a tree looks like! Oh, wow, beautiful! Wow, I've never seen anything like it! Thanks, buddy!"

"You all right in the head? That tree is nothing special."

"It is to me! Oh, wow, what a tree!"

And so on. Life had taken on whole new dimensions for M. B. *Wow* became his favorite word.

....

Spiritual insight can have the same effect on us if we will obey the Word of God. Things of God that meant nothing to us before will take on whole new meaning as we exercise faith in the Lord Jesus Christ and ask him to open our spiritual eyes.

....

M. B.'s neighbors brought him to the Pharisees, who had it in for Jesus. They took this opportunity to question the man and discredit Jesus.

"How did it happen?"

M. B. told them.

"This man can't be from God because He doesn't keep the Sabbath."

"Yes, but how could a sinner do such miracles?"

They turned to M. B. "What do you think about him?"

"He must be a prophet."

This discussion was not going the way the Pharisees

wanted it. Later in this inquisition, they tried aggressive-ness. They turned to M. B. and said, "Give the glory to God, not Jesus, for we know Jesus is an evil person."

"I don't know whether he is good or bad, but I know this: *I was blind, and now I see!*"

....

When we speak up for Christ, there will always be some who will introduce theological arguments. "What about the hea-then?" "If God is so good, how can he send people to hell?" "Where is hell, anyway?" Etc., etc. If we follow M. B.'s example and just tell what we know, God will be pleased with our witness (the results are his department). Of course God expects us to learn more and more of him every day as we read his Word, talk with him, and obey. Knowledge of him is progressive, as M. B. found out.

....

"All right, all right. Tell us again how it happened," sighed the Pharisees.

"I already told you. Why do you want to hear it again? Are you so eager to become his disciples that you can't wait to hear more?" M. B. retorted.

Now the Pharisees were angry. "We are Moses' disciples; we don't know anything about this man!" they shouted.

M. B. scratched his head, saying, "Amazing! Since the world began there has never been anyone who could open the eyes of someone born blind. If this man were not from God, he couldn't do it either."

"You are a rotten sinner, and do you teach us?!" screamed the Pharisees, and they threw M. B. out of the local synagogue.

....

Unjustified persecution might be our lot in life if we maintain a faithful witness for the Lord Jesus Christ. Are we willing to suffer a little for his sake after he has suffered so much for us?

....

Now what was poor M. B. to do?

The loving Lord Jesus knew what M. B. had suffered, so he visited him. "Do you believe in the Messiah?" he asked.

"Who is he, Lord, for I want to." This was not the ques-tion of a skeptic who was looking for reasons not to believe. This was not the question of an agnostic who had decided there was nothing to believe in. This was the question of a seeker after truth, wherever it might have led.

"You have seen him, and he is speaking to you!" replied Jesus.

As the illumination hit his open mind, M. B. cried, "Yes Lord, I believe!" And he worshiped Jesus.

38 The Hospitable Hostess

LUKE 10:38-42; JOHN 11:1-45; 12:1-8

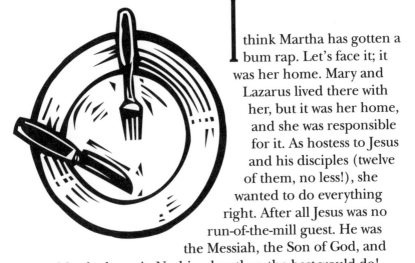

I think Martha has gotten a bum rap. Let's face it; it was her home. Mary and Lazarus lived there with her, but it was her home, and she was responsible for it. As hostess to Jesus and his disciples (twelve of them, no less!), she wanted to do everything right. After all Jesus was no run-of-the-mill guest. He was the Messiah, the Son of God, and Martha knew it. Nothing less than the best would do!

Now Martha loved Mary and Lazarus. But when it came to Mary, Martha's feelings were somewhat ambivalent. Mary was the aesthetic one; Martha, the practical one. Mary was a dreamer; Martha, a planner. Mary was the star attraction; Martha, the supporting actress. Mary had a knack for the theatrical; Martha was "plain old Martha." It was hard to always remain joyful under the circumstances.

....

Do we often feel our service to God is overlooked and unappreciated by our fellow Christians? We need to remember that God's eyes will be on the faithful ones (Ps. 101:6)! If we feel neglected, maybe the problem is not with our service but with our attitude. Are we serving for personal gratification or for God's glory?

....

On one occasion Jesus and his disciples were visiting (or should I say staying) in Martha's home in Bethany. It was a centrally located headquarters in Judea for the Savior, who had no home of his own. Martha was preparing dinner for everyone. When she took a breather, she noticed that Mary had left her assigned duties and was not to be found in the kitchen or dining room. Martha became irritated. *Just like her to wander off and leave me with all the work!*

When she found Mary *with the men,* sitting at Jesus' feet listening to him, Martha blew up. "Why are you allowing her to do this, Lord? It's not fair!"

"Martha, Martha," Jesus answered, "You are upset because you do not think I have noticed your service, aren't you? I *have* noticed, but Mary has chosen the better thing to do this time."

....

We are not told how Martha reacted. How would we have reacted? Our reactions would be excellent indicators of whether we were serving ourselves or the Savior. Sometimes we get so caught up in serving that we neglect "the better choice" of listening to God.

....

Much later, toward the end of Jesus' ministry, Lazarus died. Jesus and his disciples arrived four days later at Bethany, where Martha's home was. Mourners were much in evidence. When Martha heard that Jesus was arriving, she left the house (Mary stayed behind) and hurried to meet him outside the village gate near the tomb where Lazarus lay.

"Lord, if you had been here earlier, Lazarus would not have died," was her opening statement. "We sent you word that he was sick! But even now it may not be too late since God gives you whatever you ask."

....

Jews generally felt that a departing spirit hung around for three days, but when the fourth day arrived, that was it. No more hope. Martha's statement showed a remarkable knowledge of who Jesus was and a bountiful faith in his power. However, we need to be careful not to think that it is always

God's will to cure all sickness among believers. The "health-wealth-prosperity" gospel has no basis in a proper understanding of Scripture. Many believers have suffered greatly from disease, disability, and destitution. Even the great apostle Paul had his "thorn in the flesh." Specifically because they have suffered, these saints often display great faith in Christ and sensitivity toward others' problems.

....

Jesus gently replied, "Lazarus will rise again."

"Oh, I know that, Lord. He will rise on the Resurrection Day with everyone else!" Martha said.

"I am the one who raises the dead," Jesus continued. "Anyone who believes in me, even though he dies, shall live again. He is given eternal life for believing in me and shall never perish. Do you believe this, Martha?"

"Yes, I do," avowed Martha. "You are the Messiah, the Son of God!"

....

Did we comprehend what Martha just said? Her statement even went beyond Peter's in depth; yet Peter's "You are the Messiah, the Son of the living God" is much better known. Martha understood and believed that Jesus himself could give life, even before Lazarus was raised, while Peter had a hard time understanding it until after Jesus rose from the dead! Are we, like Martha, able to believe the statements of God's Word before we have personal experience of their truth?

....

When Mary and her attendant mourners arrived weeping, Jesus wept also. But mixed with the tears was an anger that the effects of sin on the human race were so ravaging. He asked to be shown the tomb. Then he ordered the mourners to roll away the stone from its mouth.

"Wait, Lord," the ever practical Martha intervened. "Lazarus has been dead four days. The stench will be awful!"

"Remember our conversation of a little while ago?" Jesus asked. He then commanded Lazarus to come out of the tomb, and Lazarus came.

Martha had her faults, but who does not? She was human, easy to identify with. And what an excellent example of determined faith she is!

Jesus did raise Lazarus from the grave, confirming

Martha's faith. Lazarus became the new drawing card in Bethany. Thousands of people flocked to see the man who had died and was alive again. Martha remained in the background, a faithful servant of the Lord and his people.

39 Pressed into Service

MATTHEW 27:26-32; MARK 15:15-21;
LUKE 23:26; ROMANS 16:13

Simon had traveled in to Jerusalem from his home in the country for the Passover festivities. Originally from northern Africa, he had converted to Judaism. Besides, he had heard about Jesus, the country preacher from Galilee whose activities had so angered the scribes and Pharisees. He wondered if he would have a chance to catch a glimpse of him.

On this particular day as he was navigating one of the main thoroughfares of Jerusalem, fighting through the jostling crowds, he saw a large body of people moving slowly toward him up the road. This group was not moving as a normal crowd would, but its members all seemed to be straining to see something in the middle of the pack. As the crowd enveloped Simon, he pushed ahead to try to see what was the center of attention. Suddenly he found himself on the inside edge of a clearing in the crowd. His eyes caught on the figure of a man stumbling up the street, bleeding, his beard torn from his face, and with what looked like a crown of thorns on his head, carrying a rough wooden cross on his bloody back.

As Simon watched in horror, the man stumbled again and fell. It was obvious that he could go no farther.

"Hey, you!" A rough Roman voice spoke as a heavy hand fell upon Simon's shoulder. "Get over there and carry the cross for him."

Me? Why me? Simon thought as he was shoved in the direction of the fallen man. Then he remembered that his dark skin was always noticeable among his adopted countrymen. He realized that he was powerfully built, and people often commented on how muscular he was. He just stood out in Jerusalem crowds.

"Hurry, you sluggard!" shouted the soldier, and Simon felt the butt end of a spear in his back.

As he knelt beside the man to lift the cross onto his broad shoulder, the man looked at him. In that moment Simon was captured heart and soul. The look held latent authority, appreciation, and a love for him such as Simon had never experienced before.

He proceeded to the hill called Calvary with his burden, learning along the way that the man was Jesus, the very person he had hoped to see.

....

How were we first introduced to Jesus? Often in an effort to attract others to him, we try to present him in the best possible light. We emphasize his love, his power, his ability to provide all we need, and forget to mention his humiliation, suffering, and death because of our sins. Simon met Jesus at his "worst," and unless we also "meet" him at the place called Calvary and share his suffering, our belief in him will be lopsided, selfish, and even suspect.

....

Mark, in his Gospel, tells us that this Simon of Cyrene was the father of Alexander and Rufus. That name Rufus is significant because a number of years after Jesus' crucifixion, Rufus and his mother are mentioned in Paul's letter to the Romans, written at about the same time as Mark wrote his book. And what does Paul say about Simon's wife and son? Well, Rufus was "picked out" to be the Lord's very own, and his mother had been a "mother" to Paul as well. Simon's wife and son, well known in Christian circles, were loved ones of the great apostle Paul! What happened to Simon himself? We don't know. But his meeting with Jesus on the road to Calvary had lasting effects, and future believers were blessed through knowing his family.

....

What kind of influence do we have on our families and friends? Are they drawn to Christ or repelled from him by our lives? Are we well known as "chosen ones of God"? Have we cared for other Christians as "mothers" or "fathers," counseling, comforting, and loving them as God loves us?

....

Simon of Cyrene and his family—used by God to share in his Son's suffering and to serve his church. I can't think of any better way to be remembered.

40 The Trouble with Thomas

JOHN 11:16; 14:5; 20:24-29; ACTS 1:13

Thomas tended to be pessimistic. For example, there had already been at least four attempts on the life of Jesus, two by the Jewish authorities in Jerusalem during the last year alone. Now Jesus headed in that direction again. The sad news of the death of Jesus' friend Lazarus had come a few days earlier, and Jesus wanted to go to "wake him up," whatever that meant. As the disciples were discussing the situation, Thomas said, "We might as well go along so that we may die with him."

....

It is one thing to be loyal to someone when we are optimistic about his future but quite another thing to maintain loyalty when we think we may have to die to do so. Thomas's pessimism made his loyalty more remarkable. Today in the Western world it is socially acceptable to be Christian, and we have nothing to fear (except for some teasing from friends or schoolmates). What if it was suddenly illegal to be a Christian? Would we have the strength and devotion to keep our faith in Jesus? Or would we cave in from the pressure?

....

And then there was that perplexing time in the upper room on the night that Jesus was arrested. Jesus had been talking very seriously about many things, and it seemed to

Thomas that he was getting mixed signals. Before, Jesus kept talking about his impending death. But now he was talking about going to his Father's house and preparing it for them, then coming back to take them there. Before, he had washed their feet like the lowest slave and had predicted their betrayal of him and Peter's denial. Now he was talking about going somewhere that they knew about and said that they knew how to get there. A lot of it did not make much sense. Finally Thomas had to speak up. "Lord, we don't know where you are going, so how can we know the way?"

....

At least Thomas did not give up in disgust, leave the group, and go out into the night as Judas Iscariot did. Thomas asked questions. There is nothing wrong with asking God questions. If they are asked in a spirit of true inquiry, God welcomes them. Thomas's question was the springboard for one of the most powerful statements Jesus ever made: "I am the Way, the Truth, and the Life. No one comes to the Father except through me." Don't be afraid to ask your parents or pastor honest questions about God and Christianity.

....

But lest we think that pessimism as a philosophy of life is fine, we should be reminded that it can be very costly. Because of it, Thomas missed out on what would have been the greatest experience of his life!

Jesus had been arrested, falsely tried, crucified, and buried. The disciples had fled in fear and spread apart. But now Thomas received word that the remaining disciples were going to meet again in the upper room on that first Easter night.

What's the use? he thought. *It's all over. No use beating a dead donkey. Why prolong the agony by continuing to meet together. Our group is done for. Dead. I'm not going.*

....

Have we ever felt that way about our local church? Does it seem dead, obsolete, out of touch? We should not stay away. God just might choose that meeting from which we are absent to revitalize and refresh the believers. "Not by might, nor by power, [nor by upbeat music, nor by lots of young people, nor

by dynamic preachers, etc., etc.], but by my Spirit, says the Lord Almighty" (Zech. 4:6). Also, we should look at ourselves to see if we are contributing to the deadness because unconfessed sin is a hindrance to the Holy Spirit's work in our church.

....

You can imagine Thomas's total shock when he heard, "We have seen the Lord! Really, Thomas! He came right through the closed and locked door into our midst! He even ate some food in our presence, and we did not see it going down! He wasn't a ghost, Thomas! It was really he!"

And then Thomas's old pessimism took over as he replied, "Unless I see him for myself, and feel him myself, I refuse to believe it."

But interestingly enough, the next time the disciples met, Thomas was there. He made sure that nothing kept him away!

Jesus is loving and gracious. He again appeared to them as before, but this time for Thomas's benefit especially. "Here, Thomas, see? Thomas, here, feel. Do not be faithless any longer. Believe!"

Thomas knelt before his Master, exclaiming, "My Lord and my God!"

Now listen carefully as Jesus makes a vital comment to Thomas. "You believe because you have seen me. But blessed are those who haven't seen me and believe anyway."

....

Jesus was talking about us! Unlike the disciples, we did not witness Jesus' life, death, and resurrection, so we have to trust others for their testimony. Thomas saw the proof of Jesus' resurrection; we have to trust the biblical accounts. The disciples saw the lives Jesus changed; we have to read about them in the Bible and believe the stories of those Jesus has changed today. What Jesus said to Thomas, he says to us through the Bible: "Don't be faithless any longer. Believe!"

....

41 The Benefit of Barneys
Part 1

ACTS 2:41-47; 4:36-37

W e first meet Barnabas in the early Jerusalem church. He was a shining example to that vital, dynamic, growing church.

....

It is not easy to be an example in a church of that caliber. Most of us can be examples in lifeless, listless churches that have left their first love. But in that church, in order to be used as an example, Barnabas had to be even more vital and dynamic than the others. Would God be able to hold us up as examples in that kind of church?

....

Actually Barnabas was not his real name; his Jewish parents had named him Joseph. But in that Jerusalem church he acquired the nickname of Barnabas for a special reason. In Bible days nicknames were often assigned to people based on something about their character. (We do the same thing, but physical characteristics are more commonly used, such as Red, Lefty, Doll Face, etc.) Barnabas means "Son of Encouragement," and that is what he was in that church! His encouragement of others stood out so much that whenever the Jerusalem believers thought of him, they thought, *There is a Barnabas if I ever saw one!* So Joseph became Barnabas for the rest of his life. We will call him Barney for the rest of this story.

....

In what ways do we stand out among our fellow Christians? If they were to give us a nickname in the same way that Barney received his, what would it be? Would we be a Barney or rather a Grumpy or a Lazy?

....

Barney fit right in there in Jerusalem. Even though he came from Cyprus, he settled in and felt comfortable. He made others feel comfortable also: He did not put them down, he was sympathetic to their problems, and he was loving and generous to them. Not only that, but he was full of faith and controlled by the Holy Spirit. Quite a man!

....

Would we feel comfortable in a church like that, where people are devoted to the teachings of God's Word, prayer, the Communion service, and each other? That kind of fervent religion is considered old-fashioned today. Are we such creatures of our society that we would be embarrassed to be like that?

....

Now everything in the Jerusalem church was not roses and caviar. Many of the believers were extremely poor. Some had suffered the confiscation of their property and had been blackballed because of their faith in Christ. They were in desperate straits.

Barney, concerned about people and their problems, decided he could help out. He had some land on Cyprus that he sold and brought the entire profits to the elders of the Jerusalem church to dispense to the poor as they saw fit. He attached no strings to his gift. He did not ask that a pew be labeled with his name in his honor. He did not require that the hymnbooks be stamped with "contributed by Barnabas." It was a free, voluntary gift to the Lord's people.

The result was that many others were inspired by his gift to do the same kind of thing. We read that "all the believers were of one heart and mind, and no one felt that what he owned was his own; everyone was sharing" (Acts 4:32).

....

Generosity and a willingness to share with others are two more characteristics that are becoming rare these days. When others follow our examples, are they inspired to generosity and sharing?

....

42 The Benefit of Barneys
Part 2

ACTS 9:26-31; 11:22-26

For several years Saul of Tarsus had been persecuting the church in Jerusalem with the aid of the Sanhedrin and Herod. The apostle James, John's brother, as well as Stephen, one of the Seven, had been martyred. Others had been imprisoned and beaten for the sake of Christ. One of the worst persecutors had been this Saul of Tarsus, a Pharisee who was furious that Jews were turning away from pharisaical law to become followers of Christ.

So when word arrived in Jerusalem that this same Saul had been converted to Christ on the road to Damas- cus, many disbelieved that this was possible. Is it any wonder when he arrived back in Jerusalem and tried to come to the meetings of the church that they refused him admittance? They all thought that he was using his "conversion" as a ploy to do some inside spying.

Only one believer was willing to risk checking him out. That was Barney. Apparently he visited Saul (who was later called Paul), spent time with him, questioned him regarding his new birth, and became convinced that Paul was truly saved!

One day Barney came to the meeting with Paul in tow.

He introduced Paul to the fearful believers and gave testimony of the reality of his faith. And because of Barney's character reference, Paul was welcomed and began a dynamic preaching ministry in Jerusalem to the point that finally some of his former cohorts were now out to kill him!

....

Do we have enough faith, as Barney had, that God can even save the worst of sinners? When Barney gave his character reference, it was not so much for Paul as it was for God. When others had trouble believing that God could save Paul, Barney did. We should be open to God's power so we can believe that the school bully or the atheist in gym class has been saved and then welcome him into the body of Christ.

....

Something else happened as the days went by that the Jerusalem church elders found almost impossible to believe. News came of a new church in Antioch of all places. Many believers had had to leave Jerusalem as a result of the continuing persecution; some had gone to Antioch and started gossiping the gospel there. And to Gentiles no less! Antioch was an idolatrous, immoral "Hollywood" of those days, and the same problem the Jerusalem believers had with Saul's conversion was plaguing them now. How could Gentiles in a place like Antioch really have been converted to Christ?

So the elders in Jerusalem decided they needed to investigate this situation. Guess whom they chose for the job? Of course—Barney! Off he went, and when he arrived, he was delighted to see that this Gentile church was authentic. The Holy Spirit was truly at work in their midst! So Barney did his thing there too. He encouraged them "to stay close to the Lord, whatever the cost."

Then he did a wonderful thing. Realizing that he needed help with these Gentile believers, he went to find Paul, brought him back to Antioch, and served the Lord with Paul in that church for a year, winning many to Christ and teaching them the Word of God.

....

Barney realized that his own resources were not sufficient for the task at hand. He did not get all bent out of shape but,

rather, did something positive about it. He got someone else to help him and serve with him. Have we ever refused to admit to ourselves what we know in our hearts, that we need help in serving the Lord? Do we get angry when our church leaders suggest to us that they would like us to get help or to step aside for someone else? Barney, as we will see, gradually became second banana to Saul, but together they accomplished great things for God!

....

43 The Benefit of Barneys
Part 3

ACTS 13:1–15:41; COLOSSIANS 4:10-11

I f you want something done, ask a busy person to do it" is a proverb of great truth. God believes in it. For example, "The man who uses well what he is given shall be given more. . . . But from the man who is unfaithful, even what little responsibility he has shall be taken from him" (Matt. 25:29).

In the church at Antioch Barney and Paul served as elders along with Symeon, a black man; Lucius, a Cyrenian from Africa; and Manaen, a foster brother of one of the persecuting Herods. They were all working together, serving the Lord. God called Barnabas and Paul to be the first missionaries to the Roman world! Notice Barney's progression: from an encouraging example, to an encouraging witness, to an encouraging investigator, to an encouraging evangelist, to an encouraging teacher, to an encouraging elder, to an encouraging missionary!

....

That is the way God works. As we are faithful in what he gives us to do, he gives us a little more to do, then more important service to do, etc. Faithfulness is what he is looking for in us, no matter how small or large the task.

....

On that missionary journey, a subtle change occurred. As the two men went more and more to the Gentiles, Barney began to take a backseat, and Paul became the chief speaker. Barney faded in prominence as Paul became the leader of the missionary troupe. Thus we notice that Peter is the prominent name in the first twelve chapters of Acts, and Paul takes over in the last sixteen chapters. But Barney is the bridge between the two, appearing as an important member of the body of Christ in both divisions of Acts.

....

God has a role for each of us to fill, whether it be prominent and public or secondary and supportive. The important thing is not the role but the joyful, faithful acceptance and activity in that role.

....

Barney had a nephew named John Mark, who accompanied him and Paul on the first leg of that first missionary journey. But when the going got tough, Mark got going— right back home. He was young and unprepared for the rigors of missionary life. Unfortunately, he became a bone of contention between Barney and Paul when they were planning a second missionary journey. Barney wanted to continue to work with Mark since he was the encourager, but Paul felt that Mark would be a hindrance rather than a help. Neither man would give in, so they split. Paul chose Silas, and the two went off on Paul's second missionary journey. Luke, who wrote Acts, follows their career under the inspiration of the Holy Spirit. This would seem to indicate that Paul was more right and Barnabas more wrong in their conflict.

....

We need to be careful about promoting family members to the point of division among God's people. It is good to support them, but God's work is to be done in God's way by God's chosen servants, and we should not try to thrust our opinions into God's will.

....

But once again Barney did the positive thing. Apparently he took Mark under his wing and trained and discipled him. It is thrilling to read that many years later

Mark is working with Paul again, and Paul calls him "a comfort to me." The work of Barney, the encourager, is seen in his nephew!

Barney was not perfect. At one point he got caught up in some hypocrisy being practiced by Peter (Gal. 2:13), but hypocrisy is a universal problem to Christians, so we cannot judge him too harshly. By far the overriding impression we are left with is that of a man devoted to God and God's people, spending his life in sacrificial service to his Master!

44 Risky Business

Acts 6:1-6; 8:4-8, 26-40; 21:8-9

Philip the Evangelist (Phil E. from now on) got involved with some risky business; at least it would seem so from a human perspective. But if you had asked Phil E., he would have said, "No way! I'm just following orders."

....

It is a risky business living for Christ in a world that is turning its back on him more and more. And yet, how risky can it be when Christ says such things as: "I have overcome the world," "All power is given to me in heaven and earth," and "I will never leave you nor forsake you"? We must see that, even though we might experience persecution and suffering for the sake of Christ, there is no risk involved. Even if we are martyred for his sake, we are "absent from the body, present with the Lord!"

....

Phil E. first comes to our notice as being one of the men chosen by the early Jerusalem church to oversee the extremely delicate matter of properly apportioning the food that was distributed daily among the Grecian Jewish widows and the Hebraic Jewish widows. This was not an easy job! It involved fairness, compassion, and impartiality concerning race, since the Grecian Jews were Gentiles in outlook more than they were Jews.

Is it any wonder that men who were of good reputation and full of the Holy Spirit and wisdom were needed and chosen for the job? Phil E. was one of those, willing to take on this risky work because he was under the control of the Holy Spirit. And as a result of this ministry, many in Jerusalem became Christians, even some Jewish priests.

....

Sometimes churches fall into the trap of thinking that certain jobs are not spiritual in nature and can be done by just about anybody. Wrong! Spiritual men and women, whether retired or in their teens, are needed. Also, they must be interested in doing a particular job, not grudgingly doing it because "no one else will" or because they were "guilted" into it. Are we far enough along in our spiritual lives to help in the work of the church? Let's pray that God will give us an interest in the area he would like us to serve.

....

Once the problem of the daily distribution was worked out, Phil E. went on into another risky area of service: He started preaching the gospel to Samaritans! No self-respecting Jew would even think of such a thing—unless he was controlled by the Holy Spirit. Jews had no dealings with Samaritans if they could help it. Samaritans were of a mixed blood and had a mixed-up religion. They were beneath the notice of Jewish purebloods. But Phil E. noticed them. He saw their need—their spiritual darkness. With a heart full of faith in the Lord Jesus, who had gone to Sychar's well specifically to bring a Samaritan woman to faith in himself, Phil E. took the risk of reaching out to them. The results? Crowds came to hear him preach and see the miracles he did by the power of God, and there was great revival and joy.

....

Are there any "Samaritans" that we know of that need our witness about Jesus Christ? Are we willing to risk the discomfort of putting aside our biases and reaching out to them? We might be totally amazed at the results!

....

And then one day, Phil E. received an incredible directive from God. "Leave all this revival in Samaria, and go down to the desert road between Jerusalem and Gaza." No explanation. No reason. Just go. Talk about risk taking! But how much of a risk was it? God was his

Master. God said, "Go," so Phil E. went and left the arrangements and consequences in God's hands.

At just the right place, at just the right moment (God's timing is always perfect), he met an Ethiopian official who had been to Jerusalem to worship, was returning home, and was reading a scroll of Isaiah with little understanding. He was in chapter 53, that wonderful chapter predicting the death, burial, and resurrection of our Lord Jesus Christ.

God used Phil E. to preach Jesus to him, starting at the same Scripture. The official was born again and baptized, and then went on his way rejoicing! Phil E.'s willingness to take risks this time brought an important and influential African to Christ.

....

"Theirs not to make reply, / Theirs not to reason why, / Theirs but to do and die," are the famous words from the "Charge of the Light Brigade" by Alfred, Lord Tennyson. They rode to their death because of the blunder of a commanding officer. When our Commander, Christ—who never blunders—gives us an order, do we answer back or question him? Phil E. didn't, and Christ gave him a wonderful victory over Satan through his part in the healing of an aching soul.

....

Finally, after continuing his evangelistic ministry for awhile, Phil E. took on the further risk of being a family man, opening his home to the Lord's people, and raising four daughters who grew up to be prophetesses. A whole, wholesome home resulted because Phil E. was willing to take on some risky business.

45 How to Love an Enemy

ACTS 9:1-25; 22:12-16

He's coming!"

"Here? To Damascus?"

"Here to Damascus! Why did he have to come here? Aren't there plenty of believers in Jerusalem for him to beat up?"

"How did he find out about us?"

"Who knows! What are you going to do?"

"I don't know! I have a wife and three kids! What will happen to them?"

"Why does he hate us so much?"

"Well, he doesn't hate us; he hates our Savior because he thinks Jesus is just a man who has started a new religion. He's so zealous for his Jewish law that he is determined to wipe us out since he can't get at Jesus."

"What can we do?"

"We could pray."

"For him?!"

"Well, at least that God will intervene in some way to protect our lives."

"That's the best suggestion yet. Come on, everybody; we need to pray."

So might the conversation have been in the Damascus church as the news of Saul's imminent arrival circulated.

....
What do we do when we feel threatened because of our faith in Christ? Discuss it or pray about it? God has told us to cast all our cares on him because he cares for us. Do we do it?
....

As one of the disciples named Ananias walked home, he felt somewhat comforted. He knew that his Lord was all-powerful and could do anything he wished. So Ananias committed his immediate future into God's hands, arrived home, washed up, and went to bed.

That night God came to him in a vision. "Ananias," God said. "Arise and go to Straight Street and ask at the house of Judas for Saul of Tarsus for, listen now, he is praying. In a vision he has seen you coming in and putting your hand on him so that he might receive his sight!"

"But Lord, I've heard about this man, about all the harm he has done to your saints in Jerusalem. And he's coming here with the authority to arrest us all."

"Go," said God again, "for he is my chosen vessel to bear my name before Gentiles, kings, and you Israelites. I will show him how many things he must suffer for my name's sake."

"All right, Lord, since you say so." Ananias got dressed and started out.

....
Can you imagine how Ananias must have felt as he walked toward Straight Street? How confused, thrilled, and apprehensive he must have been? Have we ever discovered in God's Word a promise that is almost too wonderful to believe? Are we willing to act upon it as though it is already fact? Since God is truly omnipotent, his promises are fact and can be depended on as though they were already history.
....

When Ananias arrived at Judas's home, all the lamps were lit, and sure enough, there was Saul, sitting, praying, and blinded by something like scales on his eyes. Not the arrogant, powerful Saul, but a humbled, dependent Saul, praying to the same Lord that Ananias did. What a miracle of love and grace!

Ananias stepped forward, placed his hands on Saul, and

beginning with "Brother Saul," continued on to tell him God's message and restore his sight. Saul never forgot those words. Years later he quoted them while giving his testimony before an angry crowd.

....

"Brother Saul!" How tender, warm, and welcoming! God did not tell Ananias to say that. It came from Ananias's own heart! Are we able to forgive and forget past fear and anger in the light of the wonderful display of God's grace? If God could forgive the one who was "persecuting him," then we, who claim to be his disciples, should do the same. It may be hard, but it is a wonderful gesture of Christian love, and it will always be remembered.

....

Ananias immediately baptized Saul and, along with Judas, introduced him to the church in Damascus. Saul spent some time there, but when his preaching infuriated many of the Jews so much they wanted to kill him, he was let down through an opening in the wall in a basket at night and escaped to Jerusalem. Ananias was probably one of the disciples who aided his escape.

....

It is one thing to recognize a fellow Christian's salvation but quite another to involve ourselves in providing for his immediate needs as a baby believer. Instruction about baptism, introduction into church life, and helping him deal with his personal problems are all a part of the nurturing process needed for spiritual growth and development. Are we willing to devote the time and effort required? Ananias was used by the Lord in the development of the greatest missionary ever! We may never be a Paul, but we can all be an Ananias.

....

46 Sewing for Souls

Acts 9:36-41

Dorcas might have been considered a dork by the worldly crowd in Joppa. Let's face it: She did not work outside her home, the poor and widows were her friends, she was a "goody-goody," and apparently she was not well physically. And more than that, she sewed. That's right, with a needle, thread, and thimble. She was just a seamstress.

The jet set of her day did not even know that she existed. She was never approached to be a spokeswoman for a nationally advertised product. She simply sat at home and sewed.

Oh, she was popular and famous to certain groups of people, though! Those widows thought she was A-number-one. The poor of Joppa would have mentioned her first if they had been asked whom they most admired. And the Christians knew who she was. She was a wonderful example of what a Christian should be, and they loved her. And most of all she was popular with God! She had devoted her life to his service and thus to the service of the least of his children. Her reward was certainly awaiting her in heaven!

....

Is our goal in life to be popular with the in crowd at school, the sophisticates at work, or the jet set at play? Are we groupies, following after famous sports, music, or media stars,

whether secular or Christian? Popularity with God often (but
not always) means unpopularity in a world that has rejected
his Son, Jesus Christ. From whom are we expecting rewards,
the world or the Savior? If it is from the world, remember what
Jesus said: "Don't do your good deeds publicly, to be admired,
for then you will lose the reward from your Father in heaven"
(Matt. 6:1).

....

One day, Dorcas died. According to the custom of
the day, her body was washed, and she was laid out in
an upper room of her home awaiting burial. The news
of this tragedy (and it *was* a tragedy to all those who
depended on her help) spread quickly.

Then someone remembered that Peter the apostle was
in Lydda, twelve miles away. The local Christians sent two
men to fetch him. I don't know what they thought he
could do, except maybe provide special comfort to the
grieving church in Joppa. Peter came immediately and was
ushered upstairs into the room where Dorcas lay. He was
surprised to find the room full of people, mostly women.

"Oh, Peter, what am I going to do? Dorcas kept my
family in clothes that I could not otherwise afford."

"She used to come and sit with my dying husband to
give me time to do the marketing. Who will do it now?"

"Look, Peter! See the beautiful work she did on this
robe? It is all I have to keep me warm at night."

"How are we going to get along without her? Why did
God have to take her so soon?"

....

If we were to die today, would there be anyone other than
family mourning our passing? Would we leave such a hole
behind that it would be almost impossible to fill? Would
anyone care? Have we been using those skills God has given
us to impact others for his glory? We can never start working
on our reputation too early.

....

Besieged by brokenhearted believers, Peter was over-
whelmed. After asking them all to leave, he threw himself
down on his knees and poured out his heart to God. He
then said to Dorcas, "Get up, Dorcas!"

Dorcas opened her eyes, saw Peter, sat up, and stood as Peter took her hand and led her down to the stunned and astonished mourners. This news spread even more quickly.

"Dorcas is alive!"

"No, I heard she was dead!"

"She was, but Peter raised her to life again!"

"No way!"

"Way! Lots of us saw her dead and now alive again!"

"Wow! Wait till I tell the neighbors!" And so on.

Many people came to faith in the Lord Jesus Christ as they heard of Dorcas's resurrection by the power of God.

....

I have often wondered why God took her and then allowed her to return. God has not seen fit to reveal any after-death experiences Dorcas may have had nor to give us any reasons for dealing with Dorcas this way. Many new believers were added to the church because of it—maybe that was one reason. At any rate, there is much that we must accept by faith, making sure that we do not try to major on areas God has chosen to keep secret from us. Let us focus on what we know.

....

47 A Career Woman Hosts a Church

ACTS 16:11-15, 38-40

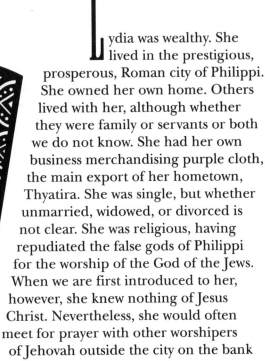

Lydia was wealthy. She lived in the prestigious, prosperous, Roman city of Philippi. She owned her own home. Others lived with her, although whether they were family or servants or both we do not know. She had her own business merchandising purple cloth, the main export of her hometown, Thyatira. She was single, but whether unmarried, widowed, or divorced is not clear. She was religious, having repudiated the false gods of Philippi for the worship of the God of the Jews. When we are first introduced to her, however, she knew nothing of Jesus Christ. Nevertheless, she would often meet for prayer with other worshipers of Jehovah outside the city on the bank of the Gangites River.

Then one day Paul, the great missionary to the Gentiles, arrived at the river, and Lydia met Christ for the first time. He changed her life.

....

There is ample evidence in Scripture that when someone is sincerely seeking after God, God knows it and will make sure that that person meets Jesus Christ. He sent a star to lead the magi to Jesus, an evangelist to the Ethiopian official in Acts

8, and Paul to Lydia. Does God see a seeking heart in us? Then he will bring someone into our lives to bring us to Christ, who is the only way to God.

....

So few Jews lived in Philippi that there was no synagogue there. Besides, Philippians in general frowned upon new religions entering their city, so prayer groups, such as Lydia's, met outside the city gates. I wonder if there were times when Lydia's business suffered a little because she did not frequent the pagan celebrations of her adopted city. Had she ever been tempted, for the sake of a larger income, to absent herself from meeting with other seekers after God to seek after money? What if she had not been there when Paul visited?

But she was! And as soon as she heard the good news about Jesus Christ, she knew she was hearing the truth. God opened her heart to receive him, and she was born again. And though she probably did not realize it, she had become Paul's first convert in Europe!

The next thing we read is that the members of her household were baptized with her. That means that when Lydia came home with the news of her salvation, they all received Christ too! Lydia's doing, perhaps? Probably.

....

Have you ever been baptized to advertise your death to sin and your resurrection to new life in Christ that lasts forever? If not, why not? If you have trusted him as Savior, what is keeping you from obeying this specific command of his? But maybe you have not yet opened your heart to him? Why not do it now and experience that deep satisfying peace of knowing you have found the Truth, Jesus Christ himself.

....

Lydia's joy overflowed in a desire to serve the Lord, and what better way than to offer the hospitality of her lovely home to the Lord's servants? When they seemed reluctant to impose on her, she would not take no for an answer. They finally agreed and found in her home a base of operations all the time they were in Philippi. Even after they were released from prison (they had been illegally incarcerated), they went back to Lydia's home to say a final good-bye to the baby Philippian church that had begun meeting there.

Lydia was an impressive woman, I'd say! Yet she would not have agreed with me. Notice the humility with which she invited Paul to her house: "If you agree that I am faithful to the Lord, come and stay at my home." Whether we are male or female, we could all be more like Lydia.

48 Total Teamwork!

Acts 18:1-3, 18-19, 24-26; Romans 16:3-5;
1 Corinthians 16:19; 2 Timothy 4:19

Aquila . . . with his wife, Priscilla." ". . . taking Priscilla and Aquila with him." "Priscilla and Aquila were there and heard [Apollos]. . . . Afterwards they met with him and explained. . . ." "Tell Priscilla and Aquila hello." "Aquila and Priscilla send you their love." "Please say hello for me to Priscilla and Aquila."

Always together! Never once named separately from the other! Working in tandem! Always a team! Husband and wife—wife and husband—perfect partners! Think of the joy that must have been theirs as they served the Lord in happy harmony!

....

When we choose a marriage partner, it is vitally important that we choose a true believer in Christ if we are Christians ourselves. "Can two walk together, unless they are agreed?" Amos asked. If we are on the narrow road to life eternal and our life partner is on the broad road to destruction, how can we possibly be on the same wavelength? And even beyond that, we must choose a true believer who is compatible with us. "Just because he is a Christian doesn't mean you should marry him" was my mother-in-law's good advice to my wife before she met me. The companionship of a compatible Christian partner is one of the greatest blessings on earth!

....

Aquila and Priscilla had not had an easy life. They had experienced racial prejudice as Jews; they had been banished from their home in Rome; they had risked their lives for the apostle Paul, and the Gentile churches knew about it and were deeply grateful to them; they had moved several times, living in distinctly different circumstances in Rome, Corinth, and Ephesus. These tensions and stresses were not conducive to maintaining one's equilibrium. Yet when two kindred spirits share them together in Christ, they divide their sorrows and multiply their joys.

....

Support groups are very popular today. The best support, however, comes from a spouse who is committed to Christ and their mate. As you look for a mate, ask yourself if this person is someone whom you can talk to and come to for encouragement and support.

....

Priscilla and Aquila were hospitable. Paul lived with them in Corinth, supporting himself as they did since all three were tentmakers by trade. In Corinth, and later back in Rome for a while, they had opened up their home for the local church to meet in. You know what that means— cleaning house before the meetings, cleaning house after the meetings, putting up with the comments of critical Christians about the decor and condition of the home.

....

Generously opening one's home to believers is one of the best ways to demonstrate the love of Christ in our lives. It requires self-sacrifice, more work, and less privacy than the norm, but the blessings that result are worth it. For example, many missionaries were once children in homes where the family had welcomed, listened to, and learned from missionaries home on furlough. Maybe we can talk to our parents about asking missionaries to stay with us on furlough or about having our youth group meet in our home.

....

Priscilla and Aquila knew their Scriptures too. They were mature believers who listened to the preachers of the Word intelligently. One of these preachers was an eloquent orator from Alexandria in Egypt named Apollos. He spoke with boldness and enthusiasm in the synagogue at Ephesus. His knowledge was limited, however, having only heard what John the Baptist had said about Jesus. After hearing him preach, this wonderful husband-wife team took him aside and taught him about "what had happened to Jesus since the time of John, and all that it meant!"

······································

Guys, when you're dating, be on the lookout for a Priscilla. Girls, keep your eyes peeled for an Aquila. It is my prayer that you will find a spouse with whom you can share your life, your interests, and your service to Christ.

······································

49 The Reliable Reporter

ACTS 20:1-4; EPHESIANS 6:21-22;
COLOSSIANS 4:7-9; 2 TIMOTHY 4:9-12

In the competition for ratings these days, the news media spout biased news that is packaged in hype, theatrics, and big smiles with pearly white teeth. How much of it can we believe? Commentators are often retracting, adjusting, or recalling former statements. The love of money has much to do with how the news is delivered. Factual, dependable, unbiased news is difficult to find.

The great apostle Paul enjoyed the fellowship of a man whom he could count on not only to give true accounts of his work to the churches but to have the wisdom of knowing what to say and what not to say. Tychicus was his name.

....

So much damage is done in Christian circles by people who are not careful about what they say to others. We would be doing well if our words can be described in this way: "A word fitly spoken is like apples of gold in settings of silver" (Prov. 25:11, NKJV).

....

Tychicus traveled with Paul sometimes, and other times he was sent on important journeys for Paul. He was a reliable investigative reporter who seemed to be able to size up a situation accurately. Several times he was sent by Paul to inform other churches of Paul's whereabouts and activities. At the same time, Paul depended on him for accurate information about the spiritual condition in those churches.

It is very difficult to form an accurate picture of how a church is doing from a short visit. The inner currents of spiritual development, the private attitudes of individuals, and personal conflicts can be hidden by the outward appearance presented at the meetings of the church. Tychicus must have been very close to the Lord and very knowledgeable about human nature to be used in this capacity. He would not jump to conclusions before all the facts were in.

....

Things are almost never as they first seem to be. Reserving judgment is very important to the unity of the church. Since we are sinners by nature, we tend to jump to negative conclusions and to assume bad motives are behind the actions of our fellow Christians. How important it is to have God's mind and direction in assessing other members of the body of Christ! We should remember that Jesus said that we would be judged to the same degree that we judge others.

....

While in prison at Rome for the sake of the gospel, Paul wrote several letters to the churches in Ephesus, Colosse, and Laodicea, as well as a personal letter to Philemon, in whose home the Colossian church met. He needed a dependable person to deliver them. There was also the matter of Onesimus, Philemon's servant, who had run away to Rome, met Paul, been saved, and was now returning to Philemon to make restitution. Tychicus was Paul's choice to be the courier of his letter to Philemon and the caretaker of Onesimus, who must have had some reservations about seeing his master.

Near the end of his life, Paul saw a need for Tychicus in the church at Ephesus. So he sent him off, even though he found it hard to do without him. Tychicus had been a "much-loved brother," a "faithful helper," and "a hard worker" as he served the Lord with Paul. Now he would use those qualities to aid the Ephesian church.

....

Can we be described as much loved, a faithful helper, and a hard worker? Or do our brothers and sisters in Christ think of us as tolerated, undependable, and lazy? Tychicus possessed qualities we all admire and hopefully want to be known for. Let's start today to try to be like Tychicus.

....

50 Tattling or Telling?

ACTS 23:12-24

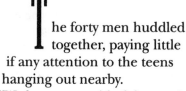

The forty men huddled together, paying little if any attention to the teens hanging out nearby.

"We have to get rid of that guy! He is trouble with a capital *T!*"

"But how?"

"Yeah, how? He's in the Roman armory! We can't get at him in there!"

"Wait a minute! I have a plan. What if we go to the chief priests and elders, tell them we want to kill Paul, and ask them to send word to the Roman commander that they want to question Paul further. Then when they are taking him to the Sanhedrin's hall, we'll jump them and kill Paul."

A short distance away, a teen started listening. He listened with both ears to the snatches of conversation coming from the group of men standing nearby. As Paul's nephew continued listening, his eyes grew wide with fear.

"But will our 'fearless leaders' agree to it?" asked one of the men.

"Of course. They hate him even more than we do. He used to be one of them until he turned traitor in favor of this Jesus character."

"Good. And just to make sure we all are committed to

this deal, let us vow not to eat or drink until Paul is dead. Yes or no?"

They vowed the vow, and after deciding the details, they disbanded, occupied by their own thoughts, oblivious to the young man running off across the marketplace.

....

Young people—little children, teens, and even young adults—are often ignored by older adults. No matter what other people think, young people have worthy and important things to say. Don't let the fact that people ignore you keep you from thinking, growing, and trying to contribute. No one is too young or unimportant for God's notice.

....

Paul's nephew arrived at the armory gate, panting and out of breath.

"Please, mister, please may I see my Uncle Paul? I need to see him quickly! Please, mister! I have to tell him something important!"

The hardened Roman soldier looked down at the earnest, pleading face. Something stirred in his heart, maybe the memory of his own son that he had not seen for many months.

"All right, sonny. Come along with me."

....

Our sovereign God can weave together timing, location, and all the insignificant experiences and emotions of our lives to work his will. It was his will that Paul be preserved to appear before Caesar in Rome. No gang of Jewish ruffians would end Paul's life before the time. Have we ever looked back over our lives to see how the seemingly disconnected events of our lives were really aligned by God to indicate his will? We should thank him for his care for us.

....

Paul's nephew spilled out what he had overheard to his uncle. Paul called an officer and said, "Take this young man to the commander. He has something important to tell him."

The officer did so. The commander listened carefully as once again Paul's nephew blurted out his story. Cautioning the boy to keep quiet and tell no one else, he sent him away. Acting quickly, he took steps to insure Paul's safety and transferred him to Caesarea and into the custody of Felix, the Roman governor. This was the first leg of Paul's long trip to Rome.

....

When is telling tattling? If we are reporting what someone did for selfish reasons, such as revenge or to avoid being punished, then maybe we should think twice before opening our mouths. But when we need to speak up to prevent harm to others, we are not tattling but helping.

....

Prayer-Wrestling

COLOSSIANS 1:3-8; 4:12-13; PHILEMON 1:23

The city of Colosse had been blessed by God indeed! Epaphras had settled there. He was God's light there. He was God's salt (a preservative and God-flavor) there. He planted God's church there. Yes, indeed, Colosse was blessed because God had directed Epaphras there.

....

Are we a blessing in our neighborhoods, or do the neighbors wish we would move? Are we a sweet-smelling aroma of Christ in our towns, or do we stink? Read on to see how Epaphras is described.

....

Epaphras had probably been saved through Paul's ministry in Ephesus and had gone to the towns of Colosse, Laodicea, and Hierapolis to preach the good news of Jesus Christ. Have you ever stopped to wonder what goes into the presentation of the gospel? First, one has to appreciate the fact that he himself is saved. Then he has to feel deeply the "lostness" of all those who are without Christ. Next he needs to pray constantly that God will use him to do everything possible to win them to Christ. Of course the study of God's Word is essential. And the "vibes" that come from him must be loving, caring ones. He needs to devote hours upon hours of time to others, befriending them, sharing and helping with their problems, counseling, and answering questions. It is hard work, but Epaphras was not afraid of hard work. So groups of Christians were born in each of these cities and met together for teaching, fellowship, the breaking of bread, and prayer. Can you imagine the thrill in Epaphras's soul as he saw the fruit of his labors?

....

What are our labors accomplishing? Will there be eternal fruit or fleeting favor? Treasures of gold, silver, and jewels or worthless sticks, hay, and straw?

....

Sadly as time went by, what happens in many churches of God's people began to happen in Laodicea and Colosse. (We do not know about Hierapolis.) Laziness in Laodicea and controversy in Colosse started creating problems. Epaphras was deeply concerned. He did not, however, wring his hands and give up. No, he fought back with all his energy. The Greek word for how he prayed is *agonizomai,* meaning to "agonize, contend, or wrestle." He agonized in prayer for his converts to Christ. He wrestled with the spiritual powers of evil for their souls. He fought against Satan's desire to have them and sift them like wheat. He really prayed!

....

Can our prayers be described by that same Greek word? What does God hear when we pray for others—a faint, feeble cry for help or a persistent, determined, dogged desire for their spiritual welfare? Do we pray until it hurts?

....

Epaphras did something else too. He made the long, arduous trip from Colosse to Rome to apprise Paul of what was happening in his beloved churches. He put himself out for them. He spent his own money. He went after the best help he could find. He really loved those people and put his love into action. The result was Paul's magnificent letter to the Colossians, defending the deity of the Lord Jesus Christ.

The Laodicean church did not fare well (see Rev. 3:14-22), but it was not Epaphras's fault. He had been faithful in the ministry that God had given to him. That

151

was all God required of him. Consequently, as he is described in God's Word, terms like "dear," "fellow servant," "faithful," "a servant of Christ," and "zealous for God's people" are used.

....

How do people in general describe us? How about fellow Christians? How about God? Can they all describe us as Epaphras is described? Wouldn't that be wonderful?

....

52 Run to Son·Light

PHILEMON 1:1-22; COLOSSIANS 4:9

Rome! The city of Caesars and the Circus Maximus! The place of the Palatine palaces! The center of the world! Rome! It filled his thoughts day and night. Days as he resentfully performed his drudgery, nights as he fell into bed exhausted and dreamed, Rome was in his head. If only he could get there—away from his servitude in Philemon's house, away from all this religious talk about some Jewish country preacher named Jesus who had died as a criminal. Why in the world would his master, who was otherwise a pretty intelligent fellow, give any credence to this new religion? Were there not enough gods and goddesses to worship already without bothering about a new one who did not sound much like a god? What kind of a god would allow himself to be killed by mere mortals?

Besides all this, the local Christ-ones met in Philemon's house every Sunday, which meant more work for him, not Philemon, although Onesimus had to admit that his master was pretty decent about pitching in. But for Onesimus, there was extra cleaning, rearranging of furniture, and food preparation to do.

Onesimus wished he could get away from it all. But he was stuck. He had no money. And even if he could get to

Rome, what could he do there with no money? No, it all looked impossible.

....

Are we dissatisfied with our station in life? Have we ever considered that God has placed us where we are according to his purpose? If we continue to kick against his restraints, we will only injure ourselves spiritually and be unable to carry out his perfect will for our lives. But maybe, like Onesimus, we are not even Christ-ones yet, having never yielded our lives to his control. If not, why not?

....

Then one day there was the money lying on the table with no one around. Almost before he realized what he was doing, Onesimus scooped it up, ran for his room, threw his few belongings together, stole out of the house, made a beeline for the nearest Rent-a-Donkey agency, and was soon on his way to Rome!

When he arrived, he was disappointed to find how little money was left, but there was still enough for him to have a good time for a few days anyway.

Time passed, the money ran out, and Onesimus needed a job. Rome had been a disappointment too. He never could feel fully a part of it all. In spite of himself, the morality of Philemon and his friends had had its effect on him, and his guilty conscience kept getting in the way of his fun. Anyway, he had to find a job. But all he knew was serving.

How they connected is not told, but eventually Onesimus did get a job, as servant to a man named Paul, who was under house arrest for something or other that was unclear at first.

Well, it wasn't long before Onesimus realized that he had jumped out of the kettle and right into the fire. Paul was a Christ-one, too, and much more knowledgeable and experienced than Philemon. Not only that, but he was one of Philemon's many friends. Onesimus could not believe it. What he had run away from seemed to have followed him to Rome, and now he was trapped again!

But as the days went by and Paul kindly and patiently

lived and chatted his Christianity, Onesimus began to watch and listen. Before long he was convicted of his sin, convinced of his need, and converted to his Savior, Jesus Christ the Son of God, from whom he had been running for so long. What relief flooded his soul! The guilt was gone. Serving others became a delight. Life become lovely. Onesimus was transformed.

....

Have we experienced the salvation that Jesus Christ offers to those who will follow Onesimus's example and run to him instead of from him? If not, we should talk to our parents, pastor, or youth leader to find out how.

....

Then Paul began to talk to Onesimus about confession and restitution to Philemon. Being reconciled to God was wonderful—but to Philemon as well? Hard—very hard! And yet Onesimus realized that if his joy was going to be totally satisfying, he had to set right what he had done. Paul was very understanding. He indicated that he would hate to lose Onesimus' services, but he would write a letter to Philemon smoothing the way home.

Onesimus did return home to Colosse and Philemon, carrying Paul's letter and one Paul had written to the church also. And much to his amazement, Philemon told Onesimus that Paul had promised to pay Philemon back for everything Onesimus had stolen! How wonderful it was to be a part of the family of God!

....

Confessing our trespasses to one another is a requirement of Christian living. Are we willing to say, "I'm sorry; will you forgive me?" and then act in such a way as to prove what we said? Restitution is also a biblical principle found throughout Scripture. It may be hard to own up to what we did and swallow our pride, but it is necessary if we really want to feel free and forgiven.

....

155

Look for this additional Bible Quest volume!

WHERE DO YOU PARK AN ARK?
Rick Blanchette 0-8423-1346-X
Historical accounts of key Bible events will help you apply important biblical lessons to contemporary life.

Additional resources for the issues in your life:

DEATH & BEYOND
James Watkins 0-8423-1278-1
The author's research and interviews with people who deal with death daily offer a biblical perspective on questions about life and death.

IF I COULD ASK GOD *ONE* QUESTION ...
Greg Johnson 0-8423-1616-7
These truthful, biblically based answers to spiritual questions will help you build a stronger faith.

IN TOUCH
Get into God's Word with these devotional excerpts from *The Living Bible*.
   Softcover 0-8423-1710-4
   Deluxe Gift Edition 0-8423-1711-2

KEEPING YOUR COOL WHILE SHARING YOUR FAITH
Greg Johnson and Susie Shellenberger 0-8423-7036-6
Advice, humor, and encouragement to guide you in sharing your faith—from authors who speak a teen's language.

SO YOU WANT SOLUTIONS 0-8423-6161-8
SO YOU WANT TO GET INTO THE RACE 0-8423-6082-4
Chuck Klein
Designed for individual or group study, these guides will help you build and live out a strong Christian faith.

WHAT HIGH SCHOOL STUDENTS SHOULD KNOW ABOUT CREATION 0-8423-7872-3
WHAT HIGH SCHOOL STUDENTS SHOULD KNOW ABOUT EVOLUTION 0-8423-7873-1
Kenneth N. Taylor
Logic and scriptural principles support a Christian viewpoint on the creation vs. evolution issue.

Fantastic!
That's what teens are saying about the *Life Application Bible for Students*. Written and edited by the nation's leading youth experts, this one-of-a-kind Bible addresses the issues you face every day. Available in *The Living Bible* and New King James Versions.